Giving Yourself Away

LARRY O'NAN

Here's Life Publishers

GIVING YOURSELF AWAY
by Lawrence W. O'Nan

Published by
HERE'S LIFE PUBLISHERS, INC.
San Bernardino, California 92402

Library of Congress Cataloging in Publication Data

O'Nan, Lawrence W., 1944-
    Giving yourself away.

    Bibliography: p.
    Includes index.
    1. Christian life--1960-   I. Title.
BV4501.2.053 1985   248.4   85-5836
ISBN 0-89840-083-X
HLP Product No. 951012

Printed in the United States of America.

FOR MORE INFORMATION, WRITE:

L.I.F.E.—P.O. Box A399, Sydney South 2000, Australia
Campus Crusade for Christ of Canada—Box 300, Vancouver, B.C., V6C 2X3, Canada
Campus Crusade for Christ—103 Friar Street, Reading RG1 1EP, Berkshire, England
Lay Institute for Evangelism—P.O. Box 8786, Auckland 3, New Zealand
Great Commission Movement of Nigeria—P.O. Box 500, Jos, Plateau State Nigeria, West Africa
Life Ministry—P.O.Box/Bus 91015, Auckland Park 2006, Republic of South Africa
Campus Crusade for Christ International—Arrowhead Springs, San Bernardino, CA 92414, U.S.A.

To my beloved wife, Pat,

who is my best friend,

wisest counsel,

greatest encourager and lover,

and partner for life!

CONTENTS

ACKNOWLEDGMENTS

My parents have been examples to me for as long as I can remember. Mom was my coach and encourager in memorizing hundreds of Scripture verses when I was a boy. Dad has provided me many illustrations and insights into the dynamics of giving. Thanks, Mom. Thanks, Dad. Thanks to both of you for giving me your love and sharing your lives with me. I love you!

Pat O'Nan, my God-given gift as my partner for life, best friend, lover, counsel and encourager, has demonstrated her commitment to this book by spending hundreds of hours typing and editing the initial manuscript. Pat, I never would have made it without your loving spirit and teamwork. Thanks! I love you!

Caroline and Jessica O'Nan, my two God-given wonderful daughters, teach me new things about living every day as they grow up into beautiful young ladies and grow in their maturity unto the Lord. Thanks, girls, for being the most precious daughters in the world! I love you!

Our many dear friends have been a faithful and vital part of our Campus Crusade for Christ team by giving their prayers and financial support. Without your constant partnership, concern, encouragement and prayers, this book never would have been written. Thanks, team, from the entire O'Nan family for your loving involvement in our lives.

Bill McConkey, pastor of the Sutter Avenue Presbyterian Church in St. Louis, Missouri, has taught me so much during our friendship of over a decade. His insight and counsel have given me a competent grasp of biblical development and a greater under-rstanding of biblical giving and receiving. Thanks, Bill, for the time you have invested in me.

Steve Douglass, vice president of administration for Campus Crusade for Christ International, has been a continuous encouragement to me, both in my responsibilities with Campus Crusade and in writing this book. His perspective and vision for this book have stimulated me to keep pressing ahead. Thanks, Steve, for giving me input during those critical times.

Bill Bright, founder and president of Campus Crusade for Christ International, continues to be an example to me of genuine way-of-life stewardship. It has been a tremendous privilege to work with him and to see him live his life in the power of the Holy Spirit. Thanks, Bill, for being an example to me.

Doug Dillard, Augie Sodaro and Bob McGregor. More than eight years ago these three friends helped me formulate this giving material into seminar outlines, aided me through considerable initial research and encouraged me to begin teaching way-of-life stewardship. Thanks, men; your labors of love have paid off!

Dave Orris, president of Here's Life Publishers, and Les Stobbe, editor of Here's Life Publishers, have encouraged me for over five years to turn my giving seminar outlines into a book. Thanks, Dave and Les, for your continued urging that has made *Giving Yourself Away* a reality.

Jean Bryant and Becky Beane, who willingly gave many hours to editing and refining the book manuscript so you the reader can focus easily on the content of the book. Thanks, Jean and Becky, for your efforts and expertise toward *Giving Yourself Away*.

Chapter 1

Pennies From Heaven

The sleepy town of Grand Junction, Colorado, awoke on Thanksgiving Day, 1947, to a fresh batch of white snow. The crisp, cool air and clear skies gave little indication of the blizzard conditions that had plagued a carload of California radio celebrities the previous night as they lumbered over three hundred miles of snow-stormed, icy, winding roads from Salt Lake, Utah. The unexpected late fall snowstorm had grounded the party's private plane.

These celebrities had left warm and sunny Southern California to fly to Grand Junction for a special Thanksgiving Day dedication of a church bell—a bell that had become, to at least 224,581 people, a symbol of hope and faith in the future. For one woman it was to be the fulfillment of her heart's desire.

In that year, 1947, Grand Junction, had been experiencing a time of building and growth after World War II. This was also true of Columbus Community Church, a small new nondenominational church just south of town, which had started in the basement of a schoolhouse. The church was the fulfillment of a dream of a few women in the Orchard Mesa community to reach neighborhood children with the good news of Jesus.

Though small nondenominational churches have always been considered bad financial risks, this had not dampened the spirits of the few members and their young pastor, his wife and their three-year-old son. Initiating a church building project, they had determined that economic realities called for an innovative approach that would involve the community. Church members went door to door "selling" bricks to their rural neighbors; people were asked to donate the price of a brick to be used in the construction of the new church.

The fund drive proved remarkably successful, getting the whole community involved in giving both money and hours of loving labor. On August 3, 1946, the community friends and members crowded into the new sanctuary to hear the young preacher deliver the dedication sermon.

In his sermon the pastor referred to the focal point of the little community church: a 40-foot-high white steeple and a belfry topped by a simple white cross. He explained that no funds were available to obtain a bell, and his one remaining desire was for a bell to ring on Sunday mornings to call the rural community to worship.

Another pastor friend was present at the dedication. That night he told his own congregation of the church dedication he had attended and of the one remaining need—a bell for the belfry.

Mrs. Helma Weber was present that evening. As her preacher spoke, God translated that new little church's need for a bell into Mrs. Weber's own personal heart's desire. While traveling home after the service, she felt that desire begin to grow, and as she turned into her driveway, she decided she must take *action*—first to pray and then to write a letter!

Among the forerunners of today's popular television giveaway shows heard in that area was a daily radio program, "Heart's Desire," broadcast by the Mutual Network stations and hosted by Uncle Ben Alexander (who later became co-star on the TV series, "Dragnet"). Each day Uncle Ben encouraged his radio audience to drop him a letter, telling him of their heart's desires.

Helma Weber felt she now had a genuine, God-given heart's desire; so, late that Sunday evening, she wrote to Uncle Ben and told him about her desire to help provide a bell for a little country church in Colorado. As she completed the letter, she prayed, then sealed the letter and mailed it to Uncle Ben the next morning.

Her letter caught the attention of the radio team. Later reflecting upon that moment, Uncle Ben commented, "I knew right then and there that the listeners of our program would want to help give that bell."

On the next radio show, Uncle Ben read Helma Weber's letter, inviting his listeners to give. He set only one limitation: the maximum contribution any individual could make was one cent!

And give America did! Pennies poured in! Interest grew. The news media carried the message worldwide, and soon pennies began arriving from other countries. Uncle Ben began calling them "pennies from heaven." Each letter contained a penny or more, and each penny seemed to have a special story behind it. In a sense, each was a gift from the heart.

There was a penny from a toddler who went without candy and dessert. Three Norwegian pilots each sent his "good luck penny" with the prayer that peace would always ring over our nation.

There were pennies from the family who thanked God for their miraculous escape in a train wreck; a penny from a mother to thank God for her newborn son; and a penny from a nurse, her symbol of participation in service to humanity. Also in the same batch of mail was a penny sent by a mother who found her gift in the chubby palm of her son after a hit-and-run driver ran him down. There was a letter from a little orphan girl who prayed, "No one ever hearing that bell will ever be as lonely as I am." Another letter contained 185 pennies—but the letter closed with 185 signatures.

Some listeners, in order to get around the one cent restriction, contributed on behalf of anyone and everyone they could think of. Two clowns (Fritz and Witz) and their trick dogs sent in nine cents—one cent for each of their dogs and for themselves. One woman sent in a penny for each state she had lived in or traveled through. One man sent in "a penny for myself, a penny for the fellow who forgot, a penny for the one who put it off, a penny for the one who lost the address, and a penny for Ben Alexander."

Creative listeners found loopholes in the contribution limitation, and the pennies kept coming. People gave because they wanted to—no one HAD to. The accumulation of pennies bought the copper and paid the craftsman to mold and pour a special copper bell, similar to those of the missions in the Southwestern states. On the bell was inscribed:

> Luke 2:14: "Glory to God in the highest and on Earth, peace good will toward all men." Into this bell has gone the pennies and prayers of 224,581 Americans of over 30 denominations, from every county in every state of the nation.

Finally the bell was completed, flown by private plane to Grand Junction and proudly installed in a specially built log cabin bell house, constructed by donated labor as members of the church hauled trees from the nearby mountains, hand stripped them and carefully laid them in place. Now all of America could see their bell.

On that icy Thanksgiving morning, Mrs. Helma Weber and 2,000 other community members bundled up and came to hear the "Heart of America" bell ring for the first time. Uncle Ben and his radio team made it over the dangerous highway from Salt Lake just in time to do an on-location "Heart's Desire" broadcast from a makeshift wooden platform in front of the little church. While the live audience waited, thousands also tuned in by radio to hear the first ring of the bell that had become their symbol of hope and peace.

The bell rang. Major newspapers gave front-page coverage to the special event. Even *True Romance* magazine carried a story of one couple's shattered lives put back together through the ringing of the bell. Governors of 32 states responded with letters and telegrams of congratulations.

Because one woman *stepped out* and took action, a God-given desire was *planted* in her heart, and 224,581 people—if only for a moment in time— gave an expression of themselves for something they viewed important.

Why did Mrs. Weber write a letter to Ben Alexander? Why did Uncle Ben choose her letter to be read to the nation over the thousands that he no doubt received? Why did 224,581 people choose to send one penny to help buy a bell for a little rural church tucked away in the hills of western Colorado?

I believe there are six important reasons you and I would also have sent our penny. Let's take a look at why we are motivated to respond to needs we see around us. As we do, let's keep in mind this basic fact: You and I *need* to give—far more than any cause needs to receive from us. God, as we will see later, made us this way.

Because we are rather complex in our thinking processes, it is important to keep in mind that not all motivations are present every time we decide to take action and give. Let me begin by asking you some soul-searching questions.

Do you give because you want to be in partnership with a worthy cause? Let's face it, we gain satisfaction from feeling a part of a worthy endeavor. Two or more people working in harmony can indeed accomplish more than one person working alone.

Some years ago, *Life* magazine released a photo story about a midwestern farmer and his family who lived next to a massive wheat field. The first photo showed the farmer and his wife panic stricken as they realized their young son was missing—nowhere to be found near the security and safety of the farm house.

The second photo indicated that the news of the missing boy had spread to the community. Neighbors had come to help search for the boy. The photo showed the confusion and distress of the people as they wandered with no direction, seeking to find the lost lad.

The third photo showed that someone had taken leadership after hours of fruitless searching. The small rural community had been organized into a human chain, each person locking hands with another, and together sweeping up and down the rows of tall ripe wheat. Each person assumed responsibility for the specific area immediately in front and to each side of him. They now had a plan in searching for the boy.

The last photo expressed heartbreak and sorrow. The father was pictured kneeling over the body of his son as those in the search party looked on in sad disbelief. Yes, they found the boy, but their effort in partnership occurred too late. He had died from exposure.

The only words in this photo feature were those of the grieving father as he looked up at the others: "I only wish we had joined hands sooner."

Partnership is joining together, locking hands in total cooperation and moving with singleness of purpose to meet an objective.

Helma Weber's request for a bell for the little country church created a sense of partnership with those who gave their pennies, each doing his part.

Do you give to meet a need? Seldom, if ever, does our human nature stimulate us to act without knowing of a need.

Recently I served as chairman for a building addition for my local church. Over a period of about two years, and in the midst of a recession, the moderately sized congregation gave over $150,000. We built only as we had the available cash. We chose never to go in debt. When the building was dedicated, the money stopped coming. Why? In the minds of those who had given, the need had been met.

After the dedication of the "Heart of America" bell in November 1947, America quit sending pennies. Why? You guessed it—there was no motivation to give. The need no longer existed.

Do you give to represent your commitment to a cause when you otherwise could not participate?

When I joined the staff of Campus Crusade for Christ in 1966, an elderly lady made a commitment to be a part of my support team through a monthly contribution of $15. She then told me why she had decided to give.

"Larry," she said, "you are doing something that I cannot do. You are going to be talking to young people of a generation different from mine. I would be frightened to be on that campus today. I would not know what to do or what to say, and I don't have the physical energy I had when I was in college. You are doing something I cannot do, so I want to help you in the only way I can—through my prayers and limited finances."

Let me tell you, those were sobering words to hear. She was trusting me to do what she was unable to do. Every month since July 1966, she has sent in her gift—216 months now of vicarious participation, totaling $3,240—on a limited income.

I'm sure that the majority of those who gave their pennies to help purchase that bell in 1947 were giving with a motive of vicarious participation. They wanted to feel a part of helping meet a need.

Do you give to satisfy your own self-worth? Have you found yourself feeling "good" inside because you gave something you had—your time, your skills, your money or personal possessions— to help meet a need?

Sad to say, many thousands of people give only with the motivation of maintaining a positive self-image. Many give because they feel it just would "look bad" if they didn't want to help.

One man confided to me some years ago, "I give to my favorite charities and donate time to worthy community projects so I have something to talk about. I would love to be free from the obligation to help; but I guess if I didn't give something, I would have trouble living with myself."

Do you give as an expression of gratitude? The one who gives with the sole motivation of expressing gratitude is rare indeed today. This person basically is saying, "I'm just thankful that I am able to help. I have been given so much, this is the least I can do."

I'm a preacher's kid. In fact, I'm the son of that young preacher who pastored that rural congregation in Grand Junction, Colorado. I remember one old gentleman who attended that little church. Mr. West was a regular. Every Sunday he drove up to church in an old Model A Ford that he kept in tip-top shape and so clean you could eat your dinner off the hood. Mr. West's health was good, but his wife was sick most of the time. His daughter, Ruth, was badly crippled from polio. Even though he and his family did not have much of the world's wealth, Mr. West was in love with the Lord Jesus and with life itself. I can still hear him say, "I can't give my God enough; He's been so good to me. He loves me so."

How many people, I wonder, who sent in pennies for the bell gave their penny out of gratitude to Jesus?

Do you give because of the blessing you will receive? I wish more people realized that blessing returns to the giver when something is given away. As a result of giving, God is able to give to the giver much more—a multiplied return on that which was given.

"I can't afford not to give, Larry," one friend said with a sparkle in her eyes. "God can bless me only if I'm giving away what He's given to me. I don't want to turn God's blessings off, so I'm going to be what He wants me to be—a pipeline that carries His love to others!"

Do you give to be remembered?

Once while visiting Washington, D.C., I decided to visit the National Cathedral. While admiring the Cathedral and learning of its history, I noticed that almost everything in the Cathedral was memorialized, in memory of a loved one.

You may have no interest in being memorialized with a monogrammed quilted kneeling cushion placed in the National Cathedral. But maybe you *would* like that friend to remember your good cooking as he cuts a slice of your freshly baked bread or piping hot pie. Otherwise, you simply would have left it on his doorstep with an anonymous note that read, "I'm thankful for you."

Do you give to achieve security? A few months ago, the families of our block began a Neighborhood Watch program. We have committed ourselves as a group to watch out for one another's property and to be alert to any activity that might be harmful to any of us. Although we aren't giving money to one another, we are committed to giving an eye or ear to what's going on around us. Why? Our security is at stake. As neighbors, we believe that if we give to one another, we can have a safer place to live.

In recent years I've met numerous men of great wealth who have chosen to give substantial sums for evangelism and discipleship. One man commented to me, "Larry, this is the only place I see to give my money. If I don't do all I can to change men's hearts through Jesus Christ, our world has no hope. I want a safe place where my grandchildren can grow to be adults. I believe that unless society is changed from the inside out there will be no security for the next generation."

Do you give for tax advantages? For over twelve years, I have given leadership to various funding thrusts on behalf of Campus Crusade for Christ. I've noticed at one particular time of the year that strange things happen: December 15-31!

This is when contributions of the strangest amounts are received— checks like the one for $5,242.50. Why? The end of the tax year was fast approaching, and the contributor had learned from his accountant that to be in a lower tax bracket, he needed to give just that much more.

Whatever their motivation for giving, when 224,581 radio listeners heard of the need for the church bell, they were willing to do something about it—in this case, send "just one penny."

But the "Heart's Desire" radio show was heard by *millions*, so why didn't more of the listeners send in their penny? What caused some to give and others not to give? Could it be that many who heard of the plan to give a penny thought, "Well, my gift won't help much," or "Sorry, Uncle Ben, I haven't got a penny to spare."

WHY WE DON'T GIVE

Could it be that the reason many of us fail to give is that we are not free to give? Is it possible that our preoccupation with things around us has paralyzed our ability to do what we know we should do?

Even Christians sometimes get caught up in the bondage of circumstances. We become paralyzed by our preoccupation with our own needs, forgetting the needs of others. Those are the times when even a penny can create a burden.

Have you ever stopped to consider seriously what it would take to change things around you? Let's face it, even if we are declared "more than conquerors" by the One who loved us, we tend to forget there are needs to be met and a world to be reached.

Today, there are more than 4.5 billion other people on this small planet. Of these, 2.7 billion have never heard the name of Jesus. If these people lined up single file, the line would circle the earth thirty times and increase in length twenty miles every day! These are people who have never had the opportunity to say yes to God's love. These people don't have a clue about why He came or what He offers them.

ARE WE IMPACTING THE WORLD?

I'm afraid we are preoccupied with our own affairs to such an extent that we fail to think about others. We in America spend $40 million each year on jigsaw puzzles. Our television sets—all 125 million of them—are on an average of six hours per day per set (we spend 164 billion hours watching TV each year). More money is spent on chewing gum and on dog food each year in the United States than on mission outreaches.

At the same time, we spend four minutes a day in prayer, while our pastors spend an average of seven minutes a day talking to our heavenly Father. Survey results show that one-fourth of all teenagers in the United States have never read a single portion of the Bible, and 50 percent of all teens cannot name even one of the Ten Commandments (only 3 percent were able to name all ten)![1]

What's the problem? It's not money. It's not ability. It's not technology. The problem is selfishness. We find ourselves in bondage to selfishness—confused, misfocused and self-seeking. We end up being responders, rather than planners. We live for the hour, forgetting we have a plan to follow. We allow our emotions and cravings for comfort to focus us on our own needs—and wants—rather than on being sensitive to the needs of others.

Dr. Richard Halverson, chaplain of the U.S. Senate, was asked by reporters for *Christianity Today* if he felt the church demonstrates a healthy exception to the "self-seekers" that surround it. His response was sobering:

> I wish I could believe that. Instead, I think the so-called worldliness of even conservative evangelicals is far more subtle than it was 25 to 50 years ago. We are badly infected with secularism, with the materialism that says, "Live for the now." Generally speaking, the people of God today are living to get as much as they can out of life this side of the grave. The eternal reference we profess in our theology we deny in our practice.
>
> For example, if you could pin people down, I think you would find very few longing for the return of Christ. His return now would instead constitute an interruption in our plans. Of course, if we had to choose, we wouldn't choose "the now" instead of eternity, but that's why the problem is so subtle. We are living without an eternal frame of reference and not even realizing it.
>
> As a result, there is very little kingdom-of-heaven interest. There is no real longing for an "awakening." God is sovereign in all these things; but to the extent that conditions have to be met for God to send an awakening like the past great

revivals, I think all the conditions have been met except one: the desire on the part of God's people for an awakening that would issue in righteousness, in selflessness, and in authentic piety.[2]

JOIN IN AN ADVENTURE

If you find yourself in Dr. Halverson's description, then I invite you to join me in an adventure to discover how to be free from our bondage to selfishness—free to care, free to reach out to others and to help meet their needs, free to give yourself away.

Mrs. Helma Weber was free. Because of her freedom, God was able to entrust to her a desire that ultimately impacted more than a quarter of a million people—and our nation, if only for a moment in time, was able to focus upon hope in the midst of selfish despair.

Has God seen fit to transfer a desire from His heart to yours? Before we begin our adventure together, take a few moments right now and focus your attention to the last page of this chapter—your first Key to Freedom exercise.

Please don't skip this important response page. Ask God to open your heart. Use your pen. As you write down your thoughts, you will begin to unlock doors that will set you free to be all God wants you to be.

KEY TO FREEDOM

Exercise One

Write down a desire you believe God has laid upon your heart. What have you seen happen to make this desire a reality?

What would you say are the three major reasons you give?

In what three areas of life would you like to experience greater freedom?

Chapter 2

Perspective From the Top

I t had been a long, exhausting week for my associate and me. We were completing our sixth straight day of teaching in Mexico. We knew very little Spanish, and our class of nineteen Latin American leaders knew very little English. Consequently, we found ourselves mentally exhausted after six ten-hour days of teaching technical material through an interpreter.

That day I dismissed the class early, sensing that they too were ready for a break.

As soon as the last member of the class was out of the room, Ricardo and Renee (the two young Mexican men who had been assigned to meet our every need) came in to get us. We had become close friends, even though language often limited our ability to communicate. Both men were in love with Jesus and demonstrated His love to us.

"Time for dinner," Renee announced. That sounded like a good idea! In my mind I pictured a quiet little cafe near the square in downtown Cuernavaca, where we could relax for an hour and then retire. But my idyllic vision exploded when Ricardo announced, "We have special evening planned. We are going to Mexico City." My heart sank! I wanted to say no, but I did not want to offend my friends. Soon my associate and I were in the back seat of an old VW Bug, and after an hour's drive, we came to the outskirts of the world's largest city. As we talked in a combination of limited English and more limited Spanish, Ricardo and Renee began to show us the sights.

Much later—after a break for dinner—we were on a walking tour in the heart of the city. My associate and I followed our two friends, with no idea where we were going.

Without warning, we made an abrupt turn into an alley, and within minutes entered a large church. The Saturday night mass was in progress, with close to two thousand worshipers in attendance.

I was hesitant to barge in, but my two hosts seemed unconcerned about disrupting the service.

We entered the sanctuary, and there I came face to face with the most beautiful giant murals I have ever seen. Each enormous painting illustrated one aspect of the life of the patron saint of Mexico, St. Francis of Assisi. I forgot that we were likely interrupting worship and stared in amazement at those dramatic works of art.

To the Mexican people, St. Francis of Assisi represents just the opposite of what the materialistic world offers them today. He was a man of great wealth and influence, but because of his concern for others, he chose to give away all he had to help meet their needs.

As I viewed the murals, I could not help but remember the prayer of St. Francis that sums up the spirit of this man:

> O divine Master,
> Grant that I may not so much
> Seek to be consoled as to console;
> To be understood as to understand;
> To be loved as to love;
> For it is in giving that we receive;
> It is in pardoning that we are pardoned; and
> It is in dying that we are born to eternal life.[1]

"Come, come, we must be going," Ricardo's voice brought me back to reality. He and Renee took the lead and we walked across the front of the church and out the door as the priest was delivering his sermon.

We followed our guides another three or four blocks. It was then we learned that we were going for a ride—straight up to the top of the tallest building in Mexico City. In minutes, our perspective on things was drastically changed. Now we were looking down on the city lights from a 32-story vantage point. As far as our eyes could see, millions of lights shone like diamonds against black velvet.

Ricardo led me to a specific spot. As we stood looking out into the darkness, Ricardo quietly said, "It was while standing here that God called me to help take His gospel to every person in my country. I gave Him my life on this spot, asking Him to use me in any way He saw fit."

Within thirty minutes, I had encountered two examples of the true biblical teaching of giving and receiving, a teaching that usually is greatly misunderstood. Francis of Assisi prayed that he would seek to give himself, rather than to be a greedy taker. Ricardo expressed his dedication to give his life so that Mexico might know his Savior.

As we rode the elevator back to the hustle and bustle of life on the street, I now knew why I was in Mexico City that night. God wanted me to grasp the significance of what it means to give yourself away.

But wait! Doesn't this giving business deal with just finances—our money? Sad to say, the vast majority of people believe that.

In our fast-paced, automated society, "giving"—even among Christians—has become identified almost solely with the "ol' buck." But according to God's perspective, giving deals with *life*. Ricardo recognized this. St. Francis of Assisi, eight hundred years ago, recognized this. Everything we have is to be given away, but too often our bondage to material possessions and desires of the world limit us in our ability to give as we should.

Jesus had a lot to say about giving and receiving. In fact, He spoke more about our relationship to material possessions, time and talents, than about any other topic. Of the thirty eight recorded parables of Jesus, nineteen of them concern our use of money, property, time and skills, and our relationships with others as we deal with these possessions.

Other New Testament writers caught what Jesus was saying. One verse in every five in the New Testament relates to this subject. Over a thousand passages in the Bible deal with personal prosperity and the use of possessions.[2] Are you aware that 1,565 Bible verses deal with the subject of giving alone?

Why is it, then, that we are not taught more about giving? I think the key reason is confusion and misunderstanding. Most pastors have never been schooled in the biblical basis of giving and receiving. Somewhere along the line, the truth on stewardship became so twisted that "Stewardship Sunday" now means "It's time for the yearly budget push."

Do you know what's happened? Satan has slipped in his worldly definition of stewardship on us. As a result we are neutralized. We are right where Satan wants us—doing only enough to get by—living selfish, defeated lives that attract virtually no one to the greatest giver of all.

How did we get into this mess, anyway? To gain perspective on our preoccupation with possessions, we need to go back to the beginning.

What is the first chapter of Genesis all about? Yes, you are right—creation. But let's look again. Although we see God creating heaven and earth, He is doing far more. The first chapter of Genesis is packed full of God dynamically *giving of Himself.* When God gives, confusion and chaos are transformed into purpose and meaning: *"When God began* creating the heavens and the earth, the earth was at first a shapeless, chaotic mass, with the Spirit of God brooding over the dark vapors" (Genesis 1:1, TLB).

God began to give of Himself in the expression of creation, and nothingness took on form and purpose. When God began to give, things began to happen:

God made light and then divided the light from darkness.

God made sky by separating vapor and *giving* the earth water.

God made dry land by *giving* the water defined parameters.

God *gave* life to the land; at His word life appeared:

And he said, "Let the earth burst forth with every sort of grass and seed-bearing plant, and fruit trees with seeds inside the fruit, so that these seeds will produce the kinds of plants and fruits they came from" (Genesis 1:11,12,TLB).

God *gave* order to the heavens by *giving* instructions:

> Then God said, "Let there be bright lights in the sky to give light to the earth and to identify the day and the night; they shall bring about the seasons on the earth, and mark the days and years." And so it was (Genesis 1:14,15,TLB).

God *gave* life to the sky and oceans by His command:

> Then God said, "Let the waters teem with fish and other life, and let the skies be filled with birds of every kind" (Genesis 1:20, TLB).

God *gave* the gift of life to the earth by His command:

> And God said, "Let the earth bring forth every kind of animal—cattle and reptiles and wildlife of every kind." And so it was (Genesis 1:24, TLB).

In six days a perfect world was given form and purpose. God was pleased, but something was missing: a manager who would oversee God's creation.

The pinnacle of God's expression of giving Himself is found in Genesis 1:26,27 when God the Father spoke to God the Son:

> Then God said, "Let us make a man—someone like ourselves, to be the master of all life upon the earth and in the skies and in the seas."
>
> So God made man like his Maker.
>
> Like God did God make man;
>
> Man and maid did he make them (TLB).

God gave His very nature and heart to man. He gave man the authority to manage on behalf of his Maker—to oversee the other gifts of God's creation.

In making man "like his Maker," God gave him those characteristics that reflected His nature and personality. He made man as an extension of Himself, with the authority to make wise decisions and the ability to reflect His Spirit, to reproduce after his kind and to reign as a child of the King.

God gave mankind a world that was made to sustain itself. It was a world of abundance. There were no "seconds," no rejects. God created *the world* with the ability to bear fruit and be replenished.

Imagine living in a perfect environment. Not too hot. Not too cold. Not too dry. Not too humid. No weeds. No backbreaking labor. A Garden of Eden. Imagine an abundance of everything to meet every need, want or desire. What a place! We can't even begin to describe such an environment because all we know about has been affected by what happened in Genesis 3.

God was operating according to a plan—He knew what He was doing. God wasn't surprised that the first days of creation were such a success.

I'm sure a theologian could develop volumes to describe all the characteristics of God's plan, but let's look at just five basic characteristics.

1. *God's plan is timeless.* Because we live our lives governed by God's gift of time, we cannot imagine living outside of time. God, however, has no problem with our limitation. From God's view, there is no beginning or ending.

Does the thought of eternity sometimes baffle you? It baffles me. From my view, it looks almost frightening. God is already living in eternity—that's home to Him. When God gave His creation the gift of time, it was to help regulate activity. Time allowed God's creation to be all He planned it to be.

2. *God's plan is built from a foundation of TRUTH.* What God says and does can be trusted. He does not change His mind when circumstances change. Truth is a part of God's character. He is steadfast, firm, constant, loyal and faithful. Truth flows from His very being. Moses described God's truth by saying He is:

> The Rock! His work is perfect,
>
> For all His ways are just;
>
> A God of faithfulness and without injustice,
>
> Righteous and upright is He (Deuteronomy 32:4, NAS).

He is the God of truth and His Word is full of commitments and promises to us. We can put our confidence in His Word.

3. *God's plan is based on giving.* The entire Bible is a record of God in action. The record shows He is a giver. God gave, and heaven and earth were formed. God gave life to Adam and gave him a beautiful mate. Even when Adam and Eve blew it, He gave

them clothing, shelter and protection.

In Genesis 3:15, God also promises He will redeem man and give him victory over the deceiver, Satan. Isn't it interesting that this victory demanded He *give* the life of His Son? As you study God's Word, you will find He continually gives to mankind.

We are the only part of His creation that can short-circuit giving! Every created gift of creation was designed to give—it has no choice. Plants give and receive; animals give and receive. Even man, as long as he lives, cannot stop giving out carbon dioxide and receiving oxygen. God designed all creation to operate by the principle of circulation. Giving first and receiving as a result of giving are as basic to life as breathing!

4. *God's plan is characterized by agape love.* Tucked away in the book of Deuteronomy 7:7,8, we find why God brought the children of Israel out of the land of Egypt. His *agape* love motivated Him to act. Moses explained His love to the generation about to cross into the Promised Land this way:

> He didn't choose you and pour out his love upon you because you were a larger nation than any other, for you were the smallest of all! It was because he loves you, and because he kept his promise to your ancestors. That is why he brought you out of slavery into Egypt with such amazing power and mighty miracles (TLB).

Unlike our expressions of love, which almost always seem to have strings attached, God's love is an exercise of His divine will. He chooses to love without cause or without an expectation of what He will receive in return.

God's love says, "I love you, no matter what you do or don't do; I love you."

God's love says, "I love you, even when you hurt Me; I will remain faithful and love you."

God's love says, "I love you so much I sent My Son to die for you."

God's love is the glue that holds His plan together: This bonding agent is stronger than any Super Glue and lasts for eternity.

Paul defines the strength of this "glue" when he writes:

> Love is patient, love is kind, and is not jealous; love does not
> brag and is not arrogant, does not act unbecomingly; it does
> not seek its own, is not provoked, does not take into account
> a wrong suffered, does not rejoice in unrighteousness, but
> rejoices with the truth; bears all things, believes all things,
> hopes all things, endures all things (1 Corinthians 13:4-7,
> NAS).

You see, this *agape* love operates independent of circumstances. God *wills* to focus His love on us. It is His love, then,
that is the motivating force behind His plan and His freedom to
give.

5. *God's plan produces peace.* I believe the seventh day of
creation was characterized by a spirit of peace. God created a
harmonious environment each day during the days of creation.
Because of peace and harmony, He was able to say, "That's good,"
to each day's creation.

Mankind lived surrounded by God's peace until the atmos-
phere drastically shifted and became strife, as recorded in Genesis
3. Since then, mankind has desperately tried to recreate a lasting
environment of peace, but his efforts have been futile.

Even we believers often get caught up in competition and
experience strife in our activities and relationships. Rather than
reflecting the inner peace that God promises His children, we
become preoccupied with circumstances, leading to disharmony
and emptiness.

The world cries for peace daily. Watch tonight's newscast.
You will probably hear the word "peace" mentioned at least once.
But the majority of the news broadcast will demonstrate chaos,
competition, emptiness, strife, loneliness and confusion. Be assured, this is NOT God's doing!

Over the centuries man has striven to create peace on his
own. But manmade programs, at best, offer brief interludes of
freedom from tension. At the United Nations, men and women
talk about, but are far from, their goal of unity and peace. Summit
talks may provide a platform of negotiations among leaders of
major powers, but distrust and opposing ideologies prevent these
meetings from producing what the world wants more than anything else—lasting peace.

Why can't man obtain peace? Because he is using the wrong process! He is trying to create peace apart from the God of peace.

God wants us to live abundant, victorious lives. Certainly He is aware of our frailties. He knows we have trouble comprehending eternity when we live in time. He knows we have trouble defining truth in a world full of deception. He knows we experience conflict in a greedy environment and have difficulty in freely giving ourselves away. He knows *agape* love is not often experienced in our relationships because of our human frailty in reflecting His love to others. He knows that the peace He gives is not what the world attempts to give.

Yes, God knows! He also knows that we can grow to understand *His* perfect perspective on these areas as we learn to live in the power of the Holy Spirit. We can be more than conquerors through the one who loved us first. We can tap the wisdom and understanding that can come only from Him.

Take some time now to reflect on your heavenly Father's view of things. Spend a few quiet minutes responding to your Key to Freedom exercise at the close of this chapter. Take time to thank God that His perspective is full of hope.

KEY TO FREEDOM

Exercise Two

Reread 1 Corinthians 13, reflecting upon it as a description of God's love for *you* personally.

List some specific ways in which God has expressed His love to you. (The greatest expression of His love, of course, was giving His own Son, Jesus Christ, to die for us.)

Chapter 3

Lost In the Fog

My wife and I were scheduled to attend a leadership retreat in the San Bernardino mountains of Southern California. We awoke that morning to a beautiful blue-sky day. Rain the day before had lasted into the night, and the early morning sun shining on the wet green foliage in our yard was a sight to behold!

As we headed toward the mountains, we realized that the storm of the night had left the San Bernardino valley but not the mountains. Black, forbidding clouds loomed ahead of us.

As we reached the first leg of our mountain climb, we caught up with the storm. Within minutes we had left the blue skies of an April spring day and were engulfed by thick mountain fog.

What a difference fog makes! While in the sunlight, we had warmth, visibility, and orientation to where we were going. Our way was bright, cheery and peaceful. But fog presented a totally different dimension. We faced a tremendous potential for danger as we drove into the thick murky shroud. We could barely see the front of our car, much less the winding narrow road that hugged the mountainside.

No longer was our focus on the retreat hideaway where we were to meet our co-workers. The conditions that surrounded us created feelings of tension, fear, helplessness and confusion.

Circumstances governed our emotions and our objective. To move ahead we had to open both car doors and watch for the white lines that marked our path. As Pat watched for the continuous line on her right, I watched for the center lines on my left. We drove at a snail's pace, trusting that no cars had stopped ahead of us; the only way we would know would be by impact!

No doubt, as a Christian, you have some understanding as to what God has planned for you. After reading the last chapter, you can see that God has a perspective from the top; God isn't caught in the fog. Knowing His view of things gives us confidence in our heavenly Father's plan, even though we understand very little of the big picture.

Wouldn't it be great to travel through life without the restriction of earthly circumstances and human frailties? Adam and Eve had a good thing going in Eden until the gray dark cloud of sin moved in over their balmy paradise.

It is important to remember that God is still working out His plan for us. He has not changed His mind even though we may have to slow down to a snail's pace at times because the fog of our circumstances makes us blind to what's ahead.

WHY ALL THE FOG?

To understand better what causes the fog around us, come with me back to the Garden of Eden.

Remember the last day of creation? Adam, as the receiver, was happy with all that God had given, including his beautiful helpmate, Eve. Their days were full of clear azure blue skies as they learned to give back to God, their Creator. Every moment of every day, they experienced peace.

God's creation lived in total harmony. No strife. No discord. No pain. No sorrow. No distrust. The result of God's giving plan was total, perfect peace.

Every evening Adam and Eve had company. The Bible tells us that God personally came to be with them—to instruct them, to have close fellowship with them. They had open, free conversation with their Creator. The love relationship they had with God gave them freedom that man never has experienced since.

In Genesis 3, we are introduced to a new game plan that would result in emptiness and disorientation. Little did Adam and Eve realize that the decisions they were about to make on a balmy afternoon in Eden would throw the world into confusion and despair.

LESSON IN GARDENING

Remember the story? Eve was out enjoying the garden, perhaps doing some raking and tidying up a bit. Adam may have been taking a nap or he may have gone "skinny dipping" in one of the refreshing ponds.

Then the craftiest of all God's creatures slid over to Eve and initiated a conversation. In their brief dialog, we are introduced to Satan's plan of *getting*. Satan looked upon all of God's magnificent creation and found only one possible place where he could gain a toehold— man's will. He went for it with all he had and put a full press attack on man's will to choose. Let's listen, from behind a bush, to an expanded version of that conversation...

"Good afternoon, Eve. My what a beautiful day! Looks like you're enjoying yourself."

"Oh, yes, Mr. Serpent, I just love my new home. Adam's out for a few minutes, and I thought I would do a little resting this afternoon."

"Really? Eve, I'm taking a garden survey today and have a few questions for you. Do you have a few minutes? Good. I hear you're not allowed to eat any of the fruit in this garden—direct orders from God. Is that right?"

"Of course we may eat, Mr. Serpent. It's only from the tree in the center of the garden that we are not to eat. God says we are not to eat it or even touch it or we will die."

"You can't be serious! That's a lie! Look, Eve, I've known God much longer than you have. Let me assure you, you won't die. You see, God knows very well that the instant you eat of that tree, you will become like Him, for your eyes will be opened. Why, you will be able to distinguish good from evil. By the way, when did He tell you that anyway?"

"Why, just last week as we walked by there on our evening stroll, He reminded us then."

"Oh, last week! Well, now I understand. Eve, didn't you notice? The fruit wasn't quite ripe then. But things are different now—I was by there earlier today, and that fruit is ripe. It's ready for picking! Come on, let's take a look."

As they approach the center of the garden, Eve says, "Yes, Serpent, it does look ripe. I can't remember if it looked this way last week."

"Eve," says the Serpent, "you need to understand—things change; conditions change. Help yourself to the best fruit basket in Eden. It's yours! Trust me. Get it. If you don't, that one—right there—is going to spoil."

"But, God said—"

"Eve, reach out and touch that soft texture and smell that aroma. No doubt about it, it tastes as good as it looks. I had one earlier today; best fruit in the garden."

"I really shouldn't—"

"Oh, go ahead—try it—you'll have one up on Adam. He's always showing you new things. Now's your chance to get ahead."

Well, you know what Scripture records. Eve was deceived. The fruit did look lovely. It would make her wise. She ate and then gave some to Adam, and he too ate. Adam wasn't going to let Eve do something that he wouldn't do!

FOGGED IN

And as they ate the fruit that day, they suddenly became aware of their nakedness. They had blown it. In an instant, they experienced separation from God, their Creator—a separation worse than physical death.

Just what did crafty Mr. Serpent pull on Eve? Satan used his famous four-point whammy. He:

1. insisted that everything is relative;
2. emphasized getting;
3. appealed to sensual responses;
4. fostered covetousness.

It's important that we understand each of Satan's primary ploys, for this same plan is used just as successfully today.

Satan insists that everything is relative. Satan knows how to confuse the issue totally; He insists that judgment is relative. Depending on the circumstances and the conditions, you can make different decisions. His plan has no room for absolutes. There is no right or wrong in relativism.

A couple of years ago, I was skimming the *Wall Street Journal*. In the midst of the business news, I found my old friend Mickey Mouse. I learned that Mickey was having trouble keeping up with our changing times.

Remember the old favorite Disney films—"Peter Pan," "Cinderella," "Mary Poppins," "Lady and the Tramp" and the cartoons of Donald Duck, Mickey and Minnie, and Pluto?

Well, have you heard of "Midnight Madness," "Tron" or "Watcher in the Wood"? These too are Disney films, but they bombed at the box office. These Disney attempts to reach today's teens were all failures. Theodore James, Jr., an entertainment industry analyst, said, "Without doubt, Disney is undergoing a traumatic experience. Disney hasn't grasped the rapidity of the moral revolution that the United States has gone through."[1]

You see, conditions have changed since Peter Pan and Tinker Bell took Wendy, Michael and John to Never Never Land. The moral revolution of the last thirty years has created a "new standard"—characterized in teen entertainment by profanity, sex and drugs. These all have gained acceptance as normal behavior.

When "Midnight Madness," a Disney comedy, was released, it looked like a pale imitation of "Animal House." But because there was not enough profanity, sex or drugs, it died within weeks of release, costing Disney $4.5 million. Relativism took its toll on a company that chose to maintain an older standard.

But wait—that's not the end of the story. As I was working on this chapter, a full-page ad in *USA Today*[2] introduced us to Touchstone Films: "The beginning of a new Disney tradition!" The ad explained that Americans want "mature" entertainment, and while Disney Pictures will continue to create "timeless classics," their new Touchstone Films will create "timely entertainment." The first release for Touchstone Films was "Splash," a spicy, romantic comedy about a fish who hooked a man—a mermaid who loves sex as much as salt water. This is Disney's way of having its cake and eating it too. Ol' Mickey has decided to live a double standard. Everything is relative.

Satan emphasizes getting. On that afternoon in Eden, Satan found that Eve's ego could be manipulated. Remember what Satan (in Genesis 3:4,5 TLB) said?

> "That's a lie!" the serpent hissed. "You'll not die! God knows very well that the instant you eat it, you will become like him, for your eyes will be opened—you will be able to distinguish good from evil!"

What a deal! Take it, Eve! This opportunity may pass. This is not a 50 percent-off sale. This is a 100 percent giveaway! Get it now!

As Eve's greed reached for the ripe fruit, Adam also was stimulated to take part and get in on the deal. Their greed was exposed. In a single act, Satan manipulated their wills, which were designed to respond freely to God. Rather than giving attention to God's plan for them, now they could see only their immediate want. They forgot who they were, why they were here and where they were going.

The world's system has a masterful marketing scheme working today. It is out to focus our attention on things around us and destroy our traditional values. In the fog we forget why we are here and live only for the present. With our focus on the present, we become fearful of the future.

A cartoon in *Time* magazine caught my attention a few years ago. Mr. and Mrs. Average American were enjoying a quiet evening at home. As he read his favorite book, she was reviewing the sales ads in their local paper. Silence was broken as she looked up to him and said, "I wonder if we shouldn't start hoarding things before it becomes unpatriotic again."

That was in 1979, but only recently did I discover that cartoonist Chan Day had created this essay of the American attitude for the *New Yorker* magazine in 1948! Strange, isn't it, that the commentary is still relevant today!

We are preoccupied with wanting more and more. We hoard and store our possessions. The more we get, the more we want.

Jesus had an encounter with a young man who was obsessed with things. The young man came to Jesus to ask a question:

"What must I do to get into heaven?" In Mark 10:19-22 (TLB), we find their conversation:

> Jesus said: "But as for your question—you know the commandments: don't kill, don't commit adultery, don't steal, don't lie, don't cheat, respect your father and mother."
>
> "Teacher," the man replied, "I've never once broken a single one of those laws."
>
> Jesus felt genuine love for this man as he looked at him. "You lack only one thing," he told him; "go and sell all you have and give the money to the poor—and you shall have treasure in heaven—and come, follow me."
>
> Then the man's face fell, and he went sadly away, for he was very rich.

This young man was so obsessed by his possessions that he was in bondage to them. By the world's standard, he lived a righteous life. He honored his parents. He apparently gained his possessions through honest business practice. No doubt he was an outstanding young upper-class business executive in Judea. He had all the nice things of life, but his possessions controlled him. When Jesus told him what to do, he left in dismay, for he could not give up what he was hoarding.

Often we look back on conversations of this type and say with a pious attitude, "Poor guy, he wasn't willing to pay the cost of following Jesus." Are we forgetting that we too often decide how we will follow Christ by what we possess? Are there things you have today that stand in your way of following Christ all the way? Is there a status in your community that you enjoy, a dream house you now own, a summer home on the lake or a hobby that is keeping you from being maximized in Kingdom business?

Don't get me wrong, things that you have are not bad—but the issue is, Who controls whom? Have you relinquished to God your rights to the many possessions God has given to you? Are you willing to give up temporal possessions for eternal gains?

Our society is caught up in a whirlwind of materialism. We simply can't seem to get enough. Like a heroine addict, we must continually support our habit by getting more. We seem to be on a continual buying spree.

In the last few years, a new business enterprise has come on the scene which enables us to enjoy getting even more. Have you noticed the phenomenal growth of the mini-storage business?

Because we have outgrown our place to store the things we collect, we can now rent space! No longer are we limited to our home storage.

Doesn't storage-mania remind you of the illustration Jesus gave in Luke 12:16? The farmer was growing so much that he created a storage problem for himself. He decided to tear down the old, small, inadequate barns and build bigger ones. That in itself might not have been wrong, but what was his motivation? He wanted to store more and then enjoy his possessions with wine, women and song. His motivation was self-centered. He expected that all he had would be there for his personal pleasure for years to come. Are we not also guilty of storing up for a time of self-centered pleasure?

The craving for more has led even to an increase in gambling. Today Americans throw away *billions* of dollars in hopes of getting more "the easy way." A few years back, only a few states permitted gambling. Now it is aggressively encouraged by many state and local governments. To be with it today, you have to have at least one lottery ticket stashed away as you "pray" that your number will be the winner. Almost daily we hear of the big winners and hope that our number will be next.

Satan uses other subtle ways too, to get us focused on getting. As we grow in affluence, many of us become preoccupied with success. During the 1960s the pursuit of success almost seemed unfashionable, but it's back in style today. Being successful in itself is not bad. God made us with a mind to excel, but often the drive for success becomes a means to stomp on others in the pursuit of self-satisfaction. When pursued to the extreme, success leaves in its wake all forms of sickness, broken families, neglected children and career disappointments.

Satan appeals to sensual responses. He is a master at using our special gifts of hearing, taste, sight, smell and feel to advance his own program of self-centeredness and greed.

God gave man his five senses so he could fully appreciate God's creation. He still desires that we experience every aspect of creation as it lives out its continuous cycles of giving and receiving. However, Satan knows that through the senses he can misdirect man into thinking only of himself and his passion for pleasure.

Eve had enjoyed the privileges of living in Eden through the senses: She *saw* the beauty; she *smelled* the fresh air and fragrance of each flower; she enjoyed the fruit of the garden as she *tasted* the lush ripe produce; she could *hear* nature singing and could also communicate with Adam and with God; and as Adam and Eve walked arm in arm and occasionally stopped to pet an animal, they *felt* closeness that reflected their oneness with each other and with nature and with God.

Once Satan is able to focus our hearts on getting, he is able to sustain our passion for more through the senses. Today his subtle persuasion keeps us reaching out for sensual satisfaction.

While driving home from work a few years ago, I came face to face with a beautiful woman clad in a skimpy white bikini. There she was in broad daylight, stretched out in all her bronze glory, smiling at me. She was at least thirty feet tall, and impossible to ignore.

The billboard that framed this alluring creature topped a building at the corner of a busy intersection. No one could miss seeing her—and no man wanted to. It was only after her beauty caught my eye that I noticed a commercial statement accompanying this dream girl: "Things go better with milk."

The medium of advertising has proved an effective accomplice for Satan in carrying out his schemes. In fact, the people in the advertising business have become masters of manipulating our senses. In order to stimulate our hoarding impulse, advertising technicians work overtime to make things as attractive as possible.

As long as the world system can keep your attention focused on pleasure and comfort, you're not likely to be effective in your Christian walk. Every form of sensual response possible is used to misdirect you and to get you to think about yourself. Beware! If you're not careful, you could walk quite innocently into Satan's web and be trapped.

Satan fosters covetousness. Satan's plan results in an unhealthy passion for self-gratification. He knows that our craving for pleasures can result in negative competition, envy and strife.

No matter where you look today, you can't help but see the result of his plan. Through the process of our trying to outdo one another, we have created discord, disunity and distrust. The result is reflected in broken family relationships, community strife, economic turmoil and political fighting. Even within our churches today, we have cliques, gossip parties, backbiting and excessive materialism. Covetousness breeds unhealthy competition that creates an accelerated spiral of greed.

On a number of occasions as I've flown a commuter flight from Los Angeles International Airport to Ontario, California, I've noticed that sections of greater Los Angeles seem to have a passion for backyard pleasure. In some areas, every single home has a pool in the backyard.

The fad probably started when one family decided that a pool would be good for the kids and their friends, so they built a basic rectangular pool. And now there are kidney-shaped pools, free-form pools, pools with covers, even pools with whirlpools. What is more amazing, however, is that seldom is anyone *in* any of these pools!

Whether we want to admit it or not, we believers often get caught up in the process of getting, as much as the nonbelievers do. Because we live in a world full of need and greed, we tend to adapt to the culture around us. Too often we end up thinking as the world thinks.

During the Here's Life America campaign in 1976, when 185 cities were involved in special evangelistic outreaches, I attended a local city funding committee meeting. I proposed that the leadership committee endeavor to raise a majority of the needed funds by challenging a few selected individuals in the community to give $5,000 or more each. I explained that this would quickly create momentum, give credibility to the efforts and help to stimulate more giving within the community.

One businessman took issue with the proposal, saying, "There isn't anyone in this city who can give $5,000. That kind of money simply is not available!"

In spite of his emotional response, the funding proposal was adopted by the committee. In fact, at the close of the meeting, the businessmen left excited and encouraged...that is, all but the first man who spoke up. He still was convinced that getting the needed finances in their city would be an uphill battle.

As we walked out of the restaurant where the meeting was held, the conversations changed to business deals and other investment opportunities. Suddenly the vocal, cautious member of the group came alive as he excitedly told us about the good deal he had found that morning. His wife's birthday was in just a few days, and for a present he had bought her a dream car—a new luxury model with plush interior and loaded with all the modern extras, for a fraction of the dealer's cost.

Our business friend also boasted that he had made a considerable savings in the deal by paying cash.

I'm not sure what went through the other men's minds that noon in the restaurant parking lot, but I couldn't help but remember the man's comment just forty-five minutes earlier: "There's no one in this city who can give $5,000." His passion for material possessions would likely prevent him from experiencing all the blessings that his Father desired to give to him.

Do you find yourself living in a fog of confusion and focus on self? Every day of our lives, the subtle appeals of the world call us, and we easily can respond without realizing that we have been trapped in a web of deceit.

Have you ever bought a new shirt or blouse simply because it was on sale, then three months later realized that you'd never even worn it because it didn't go with any of your other clothes?

Did you purchase an item for your house because you felt you *had* to have it, and now, years later, the item still sits on a shelf, unopened and unused?

Satan is doing his best to create in us an unhealthy passion for self-gratification, but he is a defeated foe. You need not be afraid. If you are a believer, he has no power over you—greater is He who is in you than he who is in the world. Being aware of his scheme can enhance your ability to counter his hassles.

Before moving on to the next chapter, complete the Key to Freedom exercise that follows. It is important for you to identify ways that you get caught in Satan's traps. Once you recognize the ploys of your enemy, you will be better prepared to counter the attack. Satan is a master of deceit, but that's no reason for us to play his games. If we learn the rules, we can be winners, not losers!

KEY TO FREEDOM
Exercise Three

Describe in your own words how you unknowingly have been caught by Satan's plan of getting. Write down three examples from your own experience.

1.

2.

3.

We all have a tendency to be impulsive at times. Jot down examples that come to your mind in the following categories—be specific:

1. While shopping:

2. While enjoying leisure time:

3. While going about your daily tasks:

Chapter 4

A Prize For A Prince

Dad pulled the old 1948 Dodge panel truck into our drive-way. My brother and I ran to meet him, eager to see what he had brought us from Arizona. Dad had an outdoor advertising business that supplemented the small salary the church paid him as pastor. He had been on a sign trip for five days, and such trips always meant something special for his two boys!

As Dad climbed out of his van, he had a special twinkle in his eyes. "Wait till you see what I've got for you," he said as he walked to the back and opened the doors of the van. Much to our amazement and shock, there stood a 38-inch-high Shetland pony!

Prince was raised in the Arizona desert near the Navajo In-dian reservation. Because of the high cost of transporting bales of hay to feed the frisky pony, the owners decided to sell their pet. Dad showed up at the right time.

Prince wasn't an ordinary pony. The little black and white fellow had been professionally trained to do tricks. He had been in at least two Hollywood westerns. Prince knew he was something special, and his neigh from inside the van seemed to proclaim proudly, "Your star has arrived!"

The little rascal was untied and bounded out of the van like a spirited toy poodle. Surrounded by Colorado sunshine and fresh green grass, Prince was in pony heaven!

Soon after Prince arrived, I learned that pony races would

be included in the June horse show. The winner would take home a shiny pair of genuine leather cowboy boots. I decided I would enter that race and win the prize.

As Prince and I "worked out" together, I found that his 38-inch height did not limit his drive and speed. How he could run!

Finally the day of the big race arrived. The event was held at an old county fairgrounds. Because the facility was seldom used, much of the property was in disrepair. The one profitable venture on the property was the huge alfalfa field inside the big oval track. The proceeds from the sale of hay kept the facility from total financial collapse.

After some other events, the loudspeaker announced, "Would the ponies and their owners prepare for the next race!" Prince and I took off for the starting gate. I was confident I would win this race. As I arrived at the starting gate, I looked up and realized for the first time that there were over two thousand people in the stands, watching. I also realized that a total of three ponies were running the race.

We lined up. Only minutes separated me from that shiny new pair of genuine leather boots. The starter gun fired, and the spectators leaped to their feet and cheered as the three ponies bolted from the gate....

Remember that big alfalfa field? Little clumps of alfalfa also grew along the edges of the race track—and that alfalfa soon caught Prince's eye. No longer was he interested in the race; he was interested in eating! Like a boy with a cookie jar, he was letting his greed get the best of him. Prince was oblivious to the other circumstances around him—including me on his back, tugging at his reins, kicking his sides and swatting his rump. I had lost control—Prince was giving in to the lure of alfalfa—and in front of two thousand spectators!

What went wrong that day? Simply this: Circumstances did not permit me to fulfill my plan. I was full of good intentions; I had practiced with Prince for days; I knew he had the ability; and I wanted those cowboy boots. But I soon discovered that good intentions and sincerity—or even ability—do not guarantee the results we expect.

Nevertheless, I believe there is a reason that things don't

always turn out as we plan: Our plans are not always *God's* plans for us. But when we understand more about His plan—and realize that He always has our best interests at heart—we can respond better to unexpected circumstances.

Let us begin by defining three words. These are often used interchangeably, but I believe it is important to understand the subtle differences in meaning. The three words are *needs, wants* and *desires*.

In general, a *need* is a lack of something required by life. Typically a need is an essential item that must be obtained in order to survive. Food, clothing and shelter fall within this definition. Needs may differ, depending on one's circumstances.

If your friend announces, "I want pizza for lunch," you understand that pizza is a preference for a type of food. Nourishment is the need; pizza is a want. Lunch could just as well be a glass of milk and a sandwich.

A *want* is a craving for something that often makes us focus our total attention on that object. A want has become extreme when obsession and impulsiveness have taken control over wisdom, understanding and waiting for God's timing.

God has promised to supply our needs. He has not promised to supply all our wants. As a loving Father, however, He often makes provision for our wants, too. I've thought about the subtle difference between these two words, and I've concluded that a need is based on God's promised provision. A want is based more on one's own self-centeredness.

I saw an example of this early one morning. Answering a knock at my front door, I found an attractive young lady on our porch. Before I was able to say, "Good morning," she started in: "Hi, I'm Jennifer. I *want* to win $1,000, and I *want* your help. I *want* to go to Bermuda on a five-day cruise; but to get on that 'love boat,' I need 20,000 points. I've got 19,000 and lack only 1,000 points to make it. I'm super greedy and *want* you to buy one of these magazines from me." She pointed to a typed sheet of paper clutched in her hand.

"Buy one of these. They are worth more points. You can get what you *want,* and I can get what I *want*." I began to explain that I really was not interested in magazines; but before I even completed my sentence, she turned and headed for my next-door neighbor's without even saying thanks or good-bye. When she learned I was not going to help meet her want, I was no longer of value to her. Her obsession was turning an attractive woman into an offensive snoot.

Aren't we all faced daily with the various enticements of life that can turn us toward total self-centeredness? Are you allowing your wants to dictate your attitudes on life, or are you recognizing them and turning them over to your heavenly Father to supply in His timing as He sees fit?

Now we come to the word *desire*. This is a deeply rooted longing in the heart for something. Typically, a desire is something that you cannot easily free your mind from thinking about.

I believe that God plants desires in His children's hearts. Many times He may give you a specific desire, with the expectation that you will take the actions necessary to see that desire become a reality.

Sometimes a desire can be something of significant spiritual value. God may have planted the desire for a loved one to find Jesus Christ as his Savior. This desire of your heart may cause you to pray, to share the desire with others, to share your testimony with the person or to invite him to church or other settings to hear the gospel. Although you may stimulate others to pray, you carry the primary desire or burden for the person's salvation.

Not all desires need to be of a highly spiritual nature. Even so, the desires that God plants always will bring glory and praise to Him when fulfilled.

Helma Weber was available for a desire to be planted when she heard of the need for a bell in the little church's steeple. God, I believe, chose Mrs. Weber to be the one who would carry that desire in her heart until it became a reality. Because she responded to the desire many thousands of people across America became involved.

God's message of love and forgiveness ultimately went forth across the nation via radio, newspapers and magazines. God saw Mrs. Weber was capable of giving Him the glory. She was an instrument that He chose to use to bring attention to Kingdom business! The Heart of America Bell still hangs today in its rustic log-cabin style bellhouse in front of the Columbus Evangelical Free Church as a testimony of a desire growing to maturity and ultimate reality.

THE UNTOLD STORY

There is another part to the Heart of America Bell story. The "Heart's Desire" radio team presented my father with a beautiful, gold-edged, pulpit Bible—the best money could buy. Uncle Ben asked Dad to select a Scripture verse from the big Bible that could be read over the radio just prior to the dedication of the bell.

My father is not known as a "random access" verse finder; but not knowing for sure what to read, he stood the giant Bible on its spine and gently let the book fall open. He then pointed randomly to a spot on the open page before him, and read aloud to the radio team: "Thou hast given him his heart's desire, And Thou hast not withheld the requests of his lips" (Psalm 21:2, NAS).

No one spoke. Each was momentarily stunned by what he had heard from God's timeless Word. It seemed that God had personally selected the same verse that He gave to his servant, King David, over three thousand years ago.

The silence was broken as a member of the radio team said, "If you read that verse on the air as the first verse ever read from that Bible, the listening audience will think we rigged the Bible. You must pick something else." My father chose another verse to be read, but he and the radio team knew that God had kept His promise to the little country church that day.

In our materialistic society, so crammed full of self-determination, it is often easy to forget that God's Word is full of promises and instructions that serve as keys to seeing God plant His desires in our hearts. Even when we find a promise, too many of us snatch it up as a "good-luck charm" but never take action and time in prayer to see that promise become the fulfilled desire of our heart. I don't know if Helma Weber claimed the promise of Psalm 21:2. As a godly woman, she may well have, with her letter to Uncle Ben as the first step in claiming that promise.

You are probably aware of another promise that God gave to David in Psalm 37:4 (NAS): "Delight yourself in the Lord, And He will give you the desires of your heart."

If you understand what God's Word says and claim His promises through demonstrated action and faithful prayer, God will do as He says. Because you are important to your heavenly Father, His desire is to fulfill those desires that He has planted in your heart.

Your responsibility is to *delight* yourself in the Lord—to focus on Him *with joy*. His provision is more than adequate to meet your every need and to flavor your day-to-day experience with the seasoning of His love and peace. You need no longer be confused about needs, wants and desires. You can relax and respond to His direction and provision.

Many of us have a tendency to sail through life by impulse. All too often we live only for the moment. Like my pony, we run from one clump of grass to the next, satiating our immediate wants with no thought of the finish line and thus no genuine sense of accomplishment.

This inclination to act without conscious thought is a by-product of our sin nature and if allowed to control our lives, it produces imbalance, selfishness, greed and fear. Let's look at each of these traits.

Imbalance. God did not design the world to experience shortage. His creation was designed to provide all needs for all living things. Yet today we see great disparity between rich and poor, between abundance and dire need.

The great plains of the United States have been blessed with abundant harvests of amber waves of grain for many years. Yet our abundance has created warehousing problems, to the extent that the government now pays farmers NOT to produce some crops because of oversupply. We don't know what to do with our plenty.

While we warehouse food, much of the world is starving. We live with an abundance of food—plenty of hamburgers and fresh fruits and vegetables, usually with enough left over at the end of our meal to feed the family dog. Yet in Africa, famine threatens 150 million lives. A long drought has produced an environment where men, women and children are starving to death. Entire villages have been abandoned as their residents forage the countryside for food.

There's no getting around it, there is tremendous imbalance in our world today.

Selfishness. There is within each of us a selfish nature that holds on to things that have little real value to us. We act like the old dog in a manger of hay—he couldn't eat the stuff, but he wasn't about to let any animal that *could* even get close to it.

Just think what would happen to the needs of the poor, or to the proclamation of the gospel, if we were not so selfish! Selfishness keeps us from reaching out to meet needs that exist around us. Are we so concerned for our own welfare that we deliberately turn our backs on the needs and concerns of others—not just in Africa, but in the close quarters of our own neighborhoods?

Greed. Greed also keeps us from reaching out to others. Greed prevents us from ever being fully satisfied. Haven't we all been through a Thanksgiving or Christmas when the entire family got together for a sumptuous feast? An abundance of food was spread before us, piping hot and tantalizing. The longer we sat around the table and visited, the more we continued to eat—and eat and eat! If you're like me, you probably ate three times more than you should have. When we are greedily focusing on our own stomachs, it's pretty hard to think of others.

Greed keeps us fighting for "our rights." Do you remember the Christmas a new doll arrived on the scene—the Cabbage Patch Kid? News reports told of adults physically *fighting* in the stores to claim possession of the coveted doll. One woman was rushed to the hospital after she was thrown to the floor and trampled by a mob of other adults who greedily bolted to the Cabbage Patch Doll display as soon as the store opened for business. I wonder how the little girls who received those dolls will one day look back on their parents' appalling behavior?

Fear. Today we live in a world fraught with fear. We're reaping the results of life characterized by man doing his own thing.

One of the fastest growing businesses today is the security business. The rise in crime creates great anxiety in our hearts, and we now go to great expense to buy a degree of peace and security.

During the Here's Life America "I found it" campaign—a nationwide media effort to spread the gospel—one of my associates was assigned to help raise needed funds in a large eastern U.S.

city. He identified a number of families of financial influence and made appointments to ask for their participation as financial sponsors.

One of his appointments was with an elderly man. On the day of their meeting, my friend and another man drove to a very exclusive part of the city and pulled into the circular driveway of a beautiful three-story brownstone house. They soon learned, however, that the house was not the man's home, but only his offices and security headquarters. They were instructed to drive around behind the brownstone and through guarded electronic gates.

Soon they climbed to the top of the hill to an enormous mansion overlooking the lush green hills and valleys. At the door they were met again by armed security guards and servants. They were ushered into the front marble hall, where alabaster walls were decorated with original Rembrandt paintings.

They visited with the elderly man in his private library. This gentleman was the heir of one of our nation's most popular food companies, and his affluence spoke out boldly from his secured surroundings. He now lived alone—the last of the "old guard."

As the men explained the Here's Life America strategy, the old gentleman was intrigued by the plan, but he refused to become involved. He told them that he no longer participated in any city affairs; in fact, he had not even left his residence in over two years. He was afraid that someone would try to kill him.

Imagine living the life of a multi-million-dollar recluse. Afraid of the world. Afraid of living. Afraid of losing his life and his possessions. He lived in continual defeat and fear—a result of imbalance, selfishness and greed! All the material riches he possessed could not buy him freedom to live in peace.

WHERE ARE YOU?

Are you one who has a clear focus on the finish line of your life, or are you wandering from one clump of grass to the next, hoping to get by somehow?

In the next chapter, we will be looking at our purpose for living. But before you can understand and fulfill God's purpose for your life, you must be sure of your personal relationship with your Creator. It's possible to put on a good act; but you know, and your heavenly Father knows, what's really inside.

If you know that inside you are really in bondage to sin, why not settle that issue right now? Admit to God the Father that you have been living in rebellion to Him, intent on doing things *your* way. Ask Him to forgive your sins and thank Him that He sent His own Son, Jesus Christ, to pay the penalty for those sins. Then, as an act of your will, put your trust in Jesus Christ as your Savior and Lord. He is waiting for you to make that decision. And the moment you do, His Holy Spirit will come into your life, cleanse you from your sin, and give you the assurance that you are now God's child for all eternity!

The decision to become a part of God's family is the most important decision you will ever make. If you have not already made that decision, make it now!

As you work through the next Key to Freedom exercise, thank God in prayer for His love and forgiveness. Thank Him for desiring the best for you. Thank Him for His cleansing power that allows you to experience His purpose for your life.

Now, are you ready to find out what your "job description" is as a child of the King? He's ready to introduce you to a way of life that will produce success and freedom that you've never before experienced!

KEY TO FREEDOM
Exercise Four

You will need a blank sheet of paper for this Exercise. Put today's date at the top. Address the paper, "Dear Father." Write the following introductory sentences: "As I examine my life, I recognize that I've been focusing on possessions, relationships and circumstances, rather than on You. I want to confess to You that the following sins have distracted me from focusing on Your best for me."

Once you have written this introductory sentence, spend 15 to 30 minutes in a quiet place where you can write down everything that God brings to your mind that has limited His ability to work His life through you. Listing out your sins will enable you to see more clearly what has created your confusion and disorientation in the direction God has for you.

When you have completed listing out everything that God brings to your mind, write the following verse across the list: But if we confess our sins to him, he can be depended on to forgive us and to cleanse us from every wrong (1 John 1:9, TLB).

This is a promise of God. He will forgive if we confess. There is no reason to live another day in confusion and disorientation. He wants to set your focus on running a race that you can win!

Once you have completed the exercise, destroy your letter. By faith, claim your forgiveness, and go on with a renewed desire to follow the Lord.

Chapter 5

Purpose For Living

I was twelve years old when my father decided it was time I began to learn what responsibility and accountability were all about. In other words, it was time for my first summer job. Dad arranged for me to work for a friend of his who owned a motel. My job was to clean the pool each morning, maintain the pool area throughout the day, mow the lawns, weed the flower beds and be a "boy Friday" for the maids as they cleaned the rooms each day.

The first day on the job, I was introduced to Jim, another boy about five years older than I. I was taking over his job, and he was assigned to train me. Jim showed me what had to be done. He explained how to clean the pool each day, how to back flush the filter and how to vacuum the pool once a week. He showed me where the lawn and garden tools were, demonstrated the proper way to do the tasks and told me what the owner expected.

I learned how to do my job by watching and working with Jim for a couple of days. His last words of instruction were the key to my success, "If you're not sure what to do or how to do something, don't hesitate to ask the boss. He wants things around here done right."

ON MY OWN

As I arrived for work the next morning, I realized that I was on my own! Within an hour, I ran into a snag with the pool filter.

I had watched Jim adjust the filter once, but for the life of me, I couldn't remember the order in which he did the procedure. At first I started to experiment, but then I remembered Jim's instruction, "Ask the boss."

I decided to find the boss and seek his assistance. Little did I realize the importance of that decision. He was waiting to see if I would "do my own thing" or rely on his experience and insight. Throughout that summer I sought out his counsel. His confidence in me grew as he saw that I would do my job effectively when I knew what was expected of me.

YOUR JOB DESCRIPTION

Are you aware that God has a job description for His children? As a representative of His kingdom, you have an important assignment. God wants you to be successful at your "job," but unless you are certain of your job description, it's difficult to carry it out effectively. Over the years, most of the Christians I've known have tried their best to live the Christian life but often end up frustrated because they are uncertain of their responsibilities and God's expectations of them.

I have found that most people are happiest when they know what to do and what is expected of them. Over the last fifteen years I've helped define and write at least two hundred job descriptions, and I've observed how liberated people become once they see in writing what they are to do. A job description is a tool that helps us focus on our purpose.

Following a typical format, I have written our job description as Christians. As you study it, you will no doubt find ways to make it more personal and specific to your particular task. But we will begin with a general overview.

STEWARD OF THE KING OF KINGS
JOB DESCRIPTION

I. *Purpose*: To manage effectively all that God chooses to entrust to me so as to bring praise and glory to His name.

II. *Scope*: Everywhere I go during my time on earth.

III. *Responsibilities*:

A. To *reflect* God's character, love and purpose to those I meet as an ambassador of His kingdom.

Standard of Performance: Act.

B. To *reproduce* God's love and power by multiplying His work in my life through the lives of others.

Standard of Performance: Act and inform.

C. To *reign* on God's behalf as He would reign, using His authority to advance His plan on earth.

Standard of Performance: Act and inform.

D. To *manage* the time, talent and treasure which God has entrusted to me each day so as to maximize His influence in this world.

Standard of Performance: Act and inform.

IV. *Expectations*:

A. To live in reliance upon the power of the Holy Spirit.

B. To respond in obedience by trusting in God's leading and direction.

C. To submit to God's judgment and leadership.

V. *Reporting Relationship*:

A. I report to my heavenly Father.

B. I am to work in harmony with other stewards so as to meet the responsibilities and expectations of the King.

Your job description declares you to be a "Steward of the King of Kings." To fully understand the various parts of the job description, it is important to define some key words.

What is meant by the term, steward? No, you're not assigned to the Love Boat! Today this word is identified with that crew member on a luxury cruise ship who is expected to outguess the passengers' needs and to wait on them hand and foot. Or maybe you think of a steward/stewardess on a jet plane, speedily distributing meals at 35,000 feet, serving beverages, plumping a pillow and generally tending to each passenger's comfort. These 20th century ideas illustrate how far we've veered from the dynamic of the biblical meaning of steward.

When God's Word was penned, a steward was one entrusted with great responsibility. Occasionally New Testament church leaders were referred to as stewards. The treasurer of the city of Corinth, which had a population of over 600,000, carried the title of steward.

In the New Testament, two different words are used for steward. One views the steward as a guardian, whose responsibilities include *guardianship* of children and *administration* of a household. In Matthew 20 Jesus speaks of the steward who was responsible to pay the workers for the tasks they performed. This steward was in charge of administrating the bringing in of the harvest. Today, we who are parents or guardians of children are stewards in that we are held accountable for the children's well-being and supervision until they become adults.

The other New Testament word for steward stresses the role of *manager,* dealing primarily with property. The owner would entrust his steward with the management of his affairs. The task included handling receipts, disbursements and related financial matters. The steward was a trustee of another person's property.

Jesus referred to stewards in several of His parables. The exact duties of a steward varied, depending on the master's needs; but almost always they involved overseeing the management and operations of the master's estate.

Therefore, it should not surprise us that every Christian is called a steward. God has entrusted responsibilities of His kingdom to you! *All* you have belongs to Him. You are a steward of *everything* you have. As I think about this, it almost overwhelms me. "My" house is not mine; it's His. The car I drive is not mine; it's His. The clothes in my closet are not mine; they are His. The food in my kitchen pantry is not mine; it's His. I am held accountable to manage all of these things, and much more, on behalf of the Owner.

There's no getting around it—you *are* a steward. The question is, what *kind* of a steward will you be? You can choose to be effective in your responsibility, always endeavoring to represent your King faithfully and honestly or you can choose to be sloppy, inefficient and unreliable in your stewardship. How effective you are is a decision you make, either by a conscious act of your will or by default.

In light of this biblical definition of what a steward is, let's look at a parable Jesus gave to illustrate stewardship responsibility:

> Again, the Kingdom of Heaven can be illustrated by the story of a man going into another country, who called together his servants and loaned them money to invest for him while he was gone.
>
> He gave $5,000 to one, $2,000 to another, and $1,000 to the last— dividing it in proportion to their abilities—and then left on his trip. The man who received the $5,000 began immediately to buy and sell with it and soon earned another $5,000. The man with $2,000 went right to work, too, and earned another $2,000.
>
> But the man who received the $1,000 dug a hole in the ground and hid the money for safekeeping.
>
> After a long time their master returned from his trip and called them to him to account for his money. The man to whom he had entrusted the $5,000 brought him $10,000.
>
> His master praised him for good work. "You have been faithful in handling this small amount," he told him, "so now I will give you many more responsibilities. Begin the joyous tasks I have assigned to you."
>
> Next came the man who had received the $2,000 with the report, "Sir, you gave me $2,000 to use, and I have doubled it."
>
> "Good work," his master said. "You are a good and faithful servant. You have been faithful over this small amount, so now I will give you much more."
>
> Then the man with the $1,000 came and said, "Sir, I knew you were a hard man, and I was afraid you would rob me of what I earned, so I hid your money in the earth and here it is!"
>
> But his master replied, "Wicked man! Lazy slave! Since you knew I would demand your profit, you should at least have put my money into the bank so I could have some interest. Take the money from this man and give it to the man with the $10,000. For the man who uses well what he is given shall be given more, and he shall have abundance. But from the man who is unfaithful, even what little responsibility he has shall be taken from him" (Matthew 25:14-29, TLB).

It is evident that the Master expects His stewards to manage and invest wisely. The first two stewards in the parable managed and invested their talent and produced a multiplied return. They chose to be accountable, wise and responsive. The third steward chose to ignore his stewardship responsibilities and he reaped severe discipline for that negligence. The Master's expectation of your stewardship is also high.

IMPLICATIONS OF YOUR JOB DESCRIPTION

Let's look over the rest of your job description. First you will find a purpose statement—a one-sentence summary of why you are being called to carry out the task. Your purpose is *to manage effectively all that God chooses to entrust to you so as to bring praise and glory to His name.*

You are called to enhance the image and clarify the focus of God's kingdom on earth. He will choose to entrust things to your management that He will not entrust to others, and vice versa. What He gives to you is not the issue, but what you do with what He gives to you to manage will make all the difference in the world.

As a result of your management you are to bring praise, glory, honor and thanks to His throne. Everything you do should be done with this question in mind: "How will what I am doing now bring glory and praise to my Father's name?" If what you are doing will not accomplish this, you'd better find something else to do.

Next on the job description you will see the term, scope. This aspect of your job description deals with where your purpose will be carried out. Your scope: *everywhere you go during your time on earth.* As a steward you don't get a day off. You are on duty twenty-four hours a day, seven days a week. This realization should influence what you do and determine what decisions you make. At times you will need to use careful discipline to accomplish your objective.

Being a steward full time does not mean you've got to be a "stuffed shirt" with no time for relaxation and pleasure. We are talking about an attitude of your heart. With the proper attitude, a steward can experience a life full of high adventure and joy.

Next on your job description you find certain responsibilities that you have as a steward. Let's look at each responsibility.

Responsibility #1: *to reflect God's character, love and purpose*

to those you meet as an ambassador of His kingdom. What do you
see when you look into a mirror? You see a reflection of your
image. A mirror is designed to produce an exact representation
of what is before it. That is its only purpose.

Similarly, your first responsibility is to live your life so as to
reflect the very nature and heart of God Himself. You are to love
as He loves. You are to express compassion as He does. You are
to be an agent for unity and peace. You are to give freely as He
has given to you. Whatever God would do, you are to do.

When people see you, do they see a reflection of your heavenly
Father? Are you walking and talking as an ambassador of the
King? Are you expressing His thoughts, His actions and His attitudes in your home, in your business, in social times and in
times of leisure?

Responsibility #2: *to reproduce God's love and power by multiplying His work in your life through the lives of others.* The
ability to reproduce after our kind is indeed a miracle. My two
daughters are a daily reminder to me of the amazing miracle of
reproduction. From our marriage union, my wife and I have repro-
duced two beautiful girls who are developing and extending our
lives together.

Your second responsibility as a steward is to reproduce after
your kind. You are in the business of influencing others in their
spiritual growth. You were born into God's family to reproduce!
There is no way to reproduce yourself without giving of yourself.
To see God's family grow means that you and I as believers must
give of ourselves to meet the needs of others. This responsibility
involves more than evangelism, although being ready to lead
another to a saving knowledge of Jesus Christ is definitely a part
of it. However, reproduction might also include giving a listening
ear to a neighbor's concern, taking a baked goody to a lonely
friend, offering an extra pair of hands to help a neighbor complete
a task. Reproduction demands a concentration of time and commitment.

SENSITIVE FLEXIBILITY

One Saturday afternoon, while waiting for my associate to
wrap up a seminar on wills and investments, I decided to use my

free time to organize a chapter of this book. I headed for a quiet spot off in the corner of a lounge. For fifteen minutes I enjoyed beautiful peace and quiet.

Then I was interrupted by a young man asking questions of another person at the far end of the room. I tried to ignore their conversation, but I couldn't. It seemed as though God were saying, "Larry, you've got the answers; I want you to give some time to answering Greg's questions. It's time for you to give; you were born to reproduce."

As I laid my work aside and went over to introduce myself to the young man, I learned that Greg was the custodian of the facility where we were holding the seminar. He was waiting for us to finish so that he could lock up the building. Since he seemed interested in learning more about the seminar, I saw an opportunity to share with him why it was so important to those in attendance.

From that point it seemed very natural to share with Greg how he could be a part of God's family by trusting Christ as his Savior. As we talked, I saw the light go on, and within fifteen minutes Greg invited Jesus into his heart as his personal Savior!

Greg seemed to be born to reproduce. Once he understood that he was now a child of God, he demonstrated a new countenance. We talked awhile, and then he was called away to take care of the facility needs. When I saw Greg again an hour later, he was explaining to his girl friend how she too could know Christ as her Savior.

By willfully choosing to give time to Greg, I was carrying out my responsibility of spiritual reproduction. My responsibility was not to see Greg decide to receive Christ as his Savior; my responsibility was simply to give my time, my ear, my mouth—my life— to be used of God. Successful witnessing (sharing Christ with others) is simply sharing Christ in the power of the Holy Spirit and leaving the results to God Himself. Spiritual reproduction, like physical reproduction, can occur only when one gives to another.

Responsibility #3: *to reign on God's behalf as He would reign, using His authority to advance His plan on earth.* The King of kings has given us the privilege of acting with His authority, and this privilege should not be taken lightly. To use effectively the authority delegated to us demands discipline and faithfulness. Those who misuse this authority suffer serious consequences. God has entrusted aspects of His business to His children, and He expects us to manage with wisdom and understanding.

In John 15:16 (TLB), Jesus said, "You didn't choose me! I chose you! I appointed you to go produce lovely fruit always, so that no matter what you ask for from the Father, using my name, he will give it to you." Jesus is emphasizing that the use of His name is the key to the believer's authority. This transferred authority means that we are expected to speak, act and make requests as if Jesus were taking the action personally. We are to act on His behalf in all our dealings.

My brother, Jerry, is a lawyer. When he first graduated from law school, he referred to his "fiduciary capacity." At the time I had no idea what he meant (and was too proud to ask!). But later I looked up this legal term in a dictionary. Fiduciary capacity refers to the degree of trust and confidence that one party can put in another to act in good faith on behalf of the first party.

When Jesus gave us authority to act using His name, He expressed His trust and confidence in us to act faithfully on His behalf. His delegated authority to us has created a fiduciary relationship with Him. And the failure to carry out the expected obligations of this relationship has serious implications.

Let's suppose a friend of yours decides to take a three-month vacation overseas and asks you to write his checks, pay his bills and represent him officially while he is away. You agree, and your friend gives you the power of attorney to act on his behalf. You have now entered into a fiduciary relationship.

Suppose that after your friend has been gone six weeks, you find yourself short of money. You then decide to "borrow" from your friend's resources by paying one of your own bills from your friend's checkbook. The moment you misuse your power of attorney, you commit forgery!

You also commit forgery when you misuse the authority given to you by your heavenly Father. The authority that comes with reigning as a child of the King carries tremendous responsibility! We are to live lives that are above reproach. God is light and in

Him there is no darkness at all, so stay out of the shade! Set your goal to live in the brightness and warmth of the SON!

Responsibility #4: *to manage the time, talent and treasure He entrusts to you each day so as to maximize His influence in the world.* In this responsibility lie the dynamics of God's stewards working together. None of us can carry out God's plan alone. We are expected to work as a team, seeking to advance the kingdom of God as a body of dedicated believers who choose to work together in harmony.

The word manage means to get things done through other people. God has designed His children to work in partnership with one another. As I put my time, education, experience, natural abilities, wealth and income-generating capabilities into circulation, another steward takes what I have given and—through his stewardship accountability of his time, talents and treasure—is able to multiply the harvest.

Managing one's time, talents and treasure demands proper planning, investing, analyzing needs, providing leadership and following up on matters. As a wise manager of your Father's possessions, you should evaluate where your time, talents and treasure can best be maximized. As a steward, you are held accountable for the multiplication of the item in which you invest, and you will be rewarded according to how wisely you invest what God entrusts to you.

I've observed that many stewards prefer to give of their treasure while they guard their time and talents almost as an act of selfishness. There was a time when churches could count on volunteers from their congregation to come out for work days to take care of needed repairs, participate in neighborhood visitation, and to do other tasks that required an investment of time and talents. But more and more it seems easier to hire someone else to do the work.

When we as stewards lock arms and freely give our time, talents and treasure to one another and to the needs of the unsaved world, we will impact the world dramatically for Christ. Are you ready and willing to manage to the glory of your Master?

You will note that each responsibility has a standard of performance, which simply tells you how to carry out that responsibility. As you *reproduce,* you are to act and also inform God in prayer as to what is happening—you are involving Him in the process of reproduction, for it is His Spirit that ultimately is the multiplier. As you *reign,* you are acting on His authority; thus, keeping Him informed as to how you use His name is only reasonable. *Managing* your time, talents and treasure is acting by faith, so it is appropriate to let Him know what you've given or in what you have invested so that His hand can be involved in the multiplied return.

You will also note that your job description includes expectations. At first glance, these expectations may seem almost overwhelming, but the first one is the key to the other two. It is: *to live in reliance upon the power of the Holy Spirit.* The disciples spent hundreds of hours of personal time with Jesus; and when they felt confused and despairing, Jesus said to them:

> In solemn truth I tell you, anyone believing in me shall do the same miracles I have done, and even greater ones, because I am going to be with the Father. You can ask him for *anything,* using my name, and I will do it, for this will bring praise to the Father because of what I, the Son, will do for you. Yes, ask *anything,* using my name, and I will do it!
>
> If you love me, obey me; and I will ask the Father and he will give you another Comforter, and he will never leave you. He is the Holy Spirit, the Spirit who leads into all truth. The world at large cannot receive him, for it isn't looking for him and doesn't recognize him. But you do, for he lives with you now and some day shall be in you. No, I will not abandon you or leave you as orphans in the storm—I will come to you (John 14:12-18, TLB).

What a powerful promise! Jesus committed Himself not just to walk *with* us but also to work His plan from *within* us. We are not left on our own to figure out how to perform the responsibilities outlined in our job description. We can be empowered by the holy, righteous, everlasting Father's Spirit. We are destined to be successful in our stewardship because of the supernatural power we have available to us.

Jesus' last words to His disciples summarized and emphasized once again the power that is present: But when the Holy Spirit has come upon you, you will receive power to testify about me with great effect...about my death and resurrection (Acts 1:8, TLB).

Later in Chapter 10, you will see how to tap the Holy Spirit's power. As you understand this key to the Christian life, you will find the freedom to be what God wants you to be: *someone who responds in obedience by trusting in God's leading and direction.*

Jesus said in John 14:15,21 (TLB): If you love me, obey me....The one who obeys me is the one who loves me; and because he loves me, my Father will love him; and I will too, and I will reveal myself to him.

TRUST AND OBEY

It is virtually impossible to obey someone you do not trust. To trust someone is to have confidence in his judgment. Therefore, *before you're willing to transfer your affairs to another, you want to see him in action.*

God has left us with a record of how He handles His affairs. God's Word is testimony of His character. He is worthy of our trust. We can have complete confidence in Him. He never has and never will do something that will create a breach of confidence.

Have you ever observed how young children respond to their parents? I'm sure the reason God gave us parental authority is to help us learn to respond to Him in loving obedience. In a happy home, there is no question of trust. As parents demonstrate love and confidence to their children, there is a reciprocal response from the children as they reflect their parents' attitude.

Learning obedience is a process. Have you ever heard a parent say, "Johnny, it's time to pick up in your room," and then seen young Johnny jump up from his game and eagerly run to tidy up his room? Not too often. Usually the response is, "O.K., I'll be there is a minute"; but thirty minutes later, Johnny still has not moved one inch toward his room, unless Mom or Dad has "encouraged" him to do so.

Why does this so often occur? Johnny is not trying to be disobedient—he's preoccupied with circumstances that cause him to be disobedient. Obedience is a matter of the will and of discipline to go in a direction that moves us away from our circumstances.

I'm sure there have been times when God asked you to do

something and, rather than being obedient, you chose to do something else that seemed to you a better alternative, based on circumstances. Learning to obey is a life-long adventure. At times it means stepping out into unknown territory, but the only way you will grow is to step out and see what God has for you. Disobedience will bring only emptiness and frustration as your priorities become disoriented.

Remember the Old Testament prophet, Jonah? Because he chose disobedience over obedience, he had to live with the consequences—three days alone in the belly of a great fish. That experience no doubt soured Jonah's taste for seafood for the rest of his life. His willful decision to disregard his stewardship responsibility cost him dearly. Although it was a whale of an adventure, it wasn't worth it!

SUBMIT

No doubt one of the most misunderstood words in our 20th century vocabulary is the word submit. Submit means to defer to another's judgment or to yield to the action, control or power of another. I will never forget the pony race I described earlier, where Prince and I "won" third place. That day as Prince satisfied his appetite on the alfalfa clumps, I tried desperately to get his attention and redirect it toward our original goal—to win the race! My prodding, however, was a waste of time. In no way would Prince submit to my leadership. He chose not to yield to my judgment.

In contrast, I've watched trained race horses run, winning races. A winning race horse is a submissive race horse. The jockey on his back gives instructions which the spectators seldom recognize. The jockey's position in the saddle and his every move while on the horse's back communicate directions to the horse. The responsive horse yields his dynamic power to the jockey's will. The horse, though much stronger and more powerful than the lightweight jockey, chooses to yield his ability and power to the wisdom and insight of the jockey.

REPORTING RELATIONSHIP

The last section of your job description defines your reporting relationship: *You report to your heavenly Father.* Isn't that great news? Your chain of command is to almighty God Himself. You don't work through some up-and-coming assistant. You report to the creator of the universe!

Why? Because He paid the price for your salvation. It cost Him the life of His Son to have you join His family as a steward. He doesn't want you reporting to anyone else. We will avoid getting mixed signals as to our responsibilities or expectations if we report to the one who designed our job in the first place.

We report to our Father by talking to Him in prayer. This toll-free line of communication is direct and never busy. You will never get a recording from a telephone operator. You are to tell Him what you are doing, how you see things and how you feel. You are to ask Him for insight, wisdom and understanding. He is ready to give counsel if you are ready to listen to Him.

His primary means of communicating to us is through His written Word. God's Word is an instruction manual for His stewards. An understanding of the manual allows you, the steward, to take decisive action that is in accordance with His will.

WORK TOGETHER

You are to work in harmony with other stewards to meet the responsibilities and expectations of the King. You are not the Lone Ranger! God never intended for one steward to do everything. His plan of action demands unity among stewards. Many hands working in harmony can accomplish far more than one or two off doing their own thing.

When I was a boy, a farmer's house burned down and he and his family had to build a new home from scratch. To accomplish the task by himself would have taken weeks of work, causing his other farm chores to suffer. So he decided to host a "house raising." On an appointed day, all of the neighboring farm families got together—the men to raise the house, the children to play, and the women to visit and prepare the food for the rest of the crew.

With fifteen to twenty ringing hammers and twice that many strong arms, what would have taken weeks or even months for one man was completed in a matter of hours. Why? Unity, harmony and focused objective. How much more we could accomplish in proclaiming the gospel and meeting the needs of others if more "house raising" activities took place within the body of Christ today! God intends for stewards to work together to accomplish their mission.

The following Key to Freedom exercise deals with ways to work in harmony with other stewards. Take some time to complete this before reading on.

Key to Freedom
Exercise Five

In each of the following categories list some way in which you can work in greater harmony with other stewards:

1. Your church:

2. Your community:

3. Your home:

4. Your job environment:

Chapter 6

My Father Owns It All

In 1867 a couple and their two-year-old son went camping. They chose a spot with a magnificent view of the Pacific Ocean a thousand feet below. Their campsite was just one of many hills on the father's Piedra Blanca Ranch, which covered over 270,000 acres and stretched along some fifty miles of the coastline. To provide some of the comforts of home, the boy's mother made sure that Persian rugs were placed on the tent floor and that appropriate antique furniture was in place; meals were always served on china with appropriate silver and crystal. A far cry from the adventure of "roughing it" most of us experience on camping trips!

The boy's father had come to California in the mid-1800s to seek his fortune. In his search he found something of value—the famous Comstock Silver Load! Overnight he turned his rags to riches. His son—William Randolph Hearst—was born with a "silver spoon" in his mouth.

By the time William reached his teens, he had developed a special love for the outdoors and especially for "Camp Hill," the site of their unusual camping experiences. He often returned to his favorite hill.

In 1919, he decided that he wanted something more permanent on "Camp Hill" so that his friends could enjoy what he so often had enjoyed as a boy. He named the hill La Cuesta Encartada—the Enchanted Hill—and set out to build a dream. At age fifty he began building his home to serve as a place of retreat and refreshment and to house his art and history collections.

The first buildings to be constructed were three "small bungalows" for guests—one overlooking the ocean, with 14 rooms; another overlooking the mountains,with 10 rooms; and a third facing the setting sun, with 18 rooms.

The main house came next, La Casa Grande. It grew to castlelike proportions, containing 100 rooms, including 38 bedrooms, 31 bathrooms, 14 sitting rooms, a kitchen, a movie theater, two libraries, a game room, a dining hall and an assembly hall.

La Casa Grande was built for the furniture it was to house. The height of the ceilings and dimensions of the rooms were built around furniture, fireplaces and ceilings—all collections dating back hundreds of years. On many of the walls were hung priceless Persian tapestries and rugs or beautifully carved paneling from castles or monasteries of another century.

The Enchanted Hill became a pleasure palace for many of the rich and famous. Most of the who's who of the world eventually made a pilgrimage to La Casa Grande. Recreation was in abundance. There was the 345,000-gallon, outdoor Neptune Pool, heated year-round for swimming pleasure and watched over by white marble statues. There were numerous horseback-riding trails, protected by more than a mile of vine-covered pergola so that riders would not have to be exposed to the hot summer sun as they enjoyed the breathtaking panoramic view. Two tennis courts topped the roof of the heated indoor Roman swimming pool which was lined with blue Venetian glass and 22-carat gold tiles.

The Enchanted Hill also housed the world's largest private zoo. On the hills around La Casa Grande roamed sixty species of grazing stock, selected from around the world.

An invitation to the ranch was a ticket to "Never Never Land." Twenty-five servants were always available to meet each guest's every need.

Over 200 telephones were installed on the rocks, trees and stumps. No matter where one was on the grounds, he was only a short distance from an open line to the world.

Delicious chef-prepared meals were offered to guests daily, and, between meals, refreshments and snacks were available on the many terraces.

In the 831-foot-long assembly room, guests could relax, dance or play ping-pong under a 400-year-old ceiling. Proper new swimming suits were available for the athletic guests, and once used could be taken home as souveniers. Lush fur coats were available for the cool evenings, but these remained at La Casa Grande when the guest left for home.

When Randolph Hearst died in 1951 at the age of 81, what did he leave behind? He left it all. He was worth an estimated $360 million at his death, despite the fact that in the early 1930s he was almost bankrupt and had to borrow money from friends to survive. An aggressive businessman, he left behind 94 enterprises and a 125-page will with specific instructions as to how to disperse his personal estate of $59,500,000.

Today San Simeon, California—Hearst Castle—is visited by over 5,000 people a day. La Cuesta Encartada is a costly reminder of a man who seemed to have it all—and in abundance! But did he? Was William Randolph Hearst wealthy? No doubt about it, he was a *rich* man. To finance the purchase of thousands of treasures and the building of his ostentatious San Simeon took more than small change! He was able to *buy* whatever he wanted.

But was he prosperous? One writer appraised him as a "selfish and ruthless person, possessed with an enormous ego. He was also a person who appeared wholly self-sufficient and who had an almost cavalier disregard for established convention."[1]

For years Hearst and his wife lived two very separate lives— she on the east coast and he on the west. Separation also meant he had limited time with his five sons. Poor health, selfishness and a less than happy family life do not constitute prosperity, which could be defined as having all of one's needs met and the freedom to *enjoy* that condition in abundance. Prosperity cannot be totaled on a calculator. It is a condition of life, not a balance sheet. From God's point of view, I believe Mr. Hearst was a man of definitely limited resources.

God our Father is the one who is genuinely wealthy. He has an unlimited supply of resources. He has chosen to give His wealth to His children. As we learned earlier, we have a fiduciary responsibility to manage His wealth in a way that will bring glory and honor to Him. God expects His wealth to be in constant circulation.

During an Easter vacation, my wife and I took our two daughters to tour San Simeon. As we departed from the Enchanted Hill under the brilliant glow of the setting sun, I thought, *A man once lived here who had gained the whole world—power, influence, prestige, fame, riches. But was he all he could have been? Was he a wise steward for the King of kings?* That's something to think about....

WISE AND WEALTHY

Many years ago a wise and wealthy steward moved on a God-given desire. He envisioned the construction of a temple that would be a physical reminder of God's presence with His people. Although he never saw the temple built, King David prepared the blueprints, raised the funds and then gave instructions to another wise and wealthy steward—his son, Solomon—to build what God had led David to design.

The task before Solomon was enormous! As a steward he was responsible to build the temple of God. David instructed Solomon:

> Be strong and courageous and get to work. Don't be frightened by the size of the task, for the Lord my God is with you; He will not forsake you. He will see to it that everything is finished correctly (1 Chronicles 28:20, TLB).

The temple of God would make San Simeon look like low-class government housing. David said this about his involvement:

> Using every resource at my command, I have gathered as much as I could for building it—enough gold, silver, bronze, iron, wood, and great quantities of onyx, other precious stones, costly jewels, and marble. And now, because of my devotion to the Temple of God, I am giving all of my own private treasures to aid in the construction. This is in addition to the building materials I have already collected. These personal contributions consist of $85,000,000 worth of gold from Ophir and $20,000,000 worth of purest silver to be used for overlaying the walls of the buildings. This will be used for the articles made of gold and silver and for artistic decorations. Now then, who will follow my example? Who will give himself and all that he has to the Lord? (1 Chronicles 29:2-5).

David's example of wealth distribution stimulated more giving! The leaders of Israel took the obedient steward's challenge and followed his example seriously:

> The clan leaders, the heads of the tribes, the army officers, and the administrative officers of the king pledged $145 million in gold; $50,000 in foreign currency; $30,000,000 in silver; 800 tons of bronze; 4,600 tons of iron. They also contributed great amounts of jewelry which were deposited at the Temple treasury (1 Chronicles 29:6-8, TLB).

David's wise distribution of the wealth God had given him to manage stimulated a multiplied harvest of obedient stewardship. Were the people excited about giving? God's Word records: "Everyone was excited and happy for this opportunity of service, and King David was moved with deep joy" (1 Chronicles 29:9, TLB).

David lived his life according to biblical principles. Because he was faithful in following God's principles, he had the benefit of many by-products, including peace of heart, riches, prosperity, respect, honor, wisdom and understanding.

David by no means lived a perfect life. His adulterous affair with Bathsheba and the murder of her husband, Uriah, were serious crimes. But even though David's life was scarred by sin, his heart longed to be obedient to God. Notice what he prayed after the prophet Nathan proclaimed God's judgment on David for these sins:

> O loving and kind God, have mercy. Have pity upon me and take away the awful stain of my transgressions. Oh, wash me, cleanse me from this guilt. Let me be pure again. For I admit my shameful deed—it haunts me day and night. It is against you and you alone I sinned, and did this terrible thing. You saw it all, and your sentence against me is just. But I was born a sinner, yes, from the moment my mother conceived me. You deserve honesty from the heart; yes, utter sincerity, and truthfulness. Oh, give me this wisdom (Psalm 51:1-6, TLB).

Throughout David's life he was loyal to his heavenly Father. Yes, he sinned tragically, but he was able to admit wrong. His focus was on his God. There is no record of David worshiping other gods. His heart was desirous of serving God and obeying His principles. He was a man after God's own heart (1 Samuel 13:14; Acts 13:22, NAS).

GOD'S DESIRE FOR YOU

Are you aware that God desires your life to be characterized by wealth and prosperity (and remember, this means far more than having a lot of money)? His plan for you includes having all of your needs met and the freedom to enjoy this condition in abundance. In fact, He wants you to live your life in reliance upon His unlimited supply of resources. Are you living this way now? Are you living your life according to God's principles of giving and receiving?

As I study God's Word, I see five basic principles which govern God's wealth distribution to His children. As a Christian you have the privilege of writing checks, so to speak, from God's account. However, to use this privilege, you need to understand the principles of His distribution network.

GOD'S PRINCIPLES OF WEALTH DISTRIBUTION

1. GOD, OUR FATHER, OWNS AN INFINITE SUPPLY OF EVERYTHING THAT WE, OR ANYONE ELSE, COULD EVER NEED, WANT OR DESIRE.

2. GOD HAS AN HILARIOUS TIME CIRCULATING HIS WEALTH AND RESOURCES AND WANTS HIS CHILDREN TO SHARE IN THIS PLEASURE.

3. IT PLEASES GOD WHEN HIS CHILDREN ASK FOR, THEN DILIGENTLY SEEK, SOME OF THEIR INHERITANCE SO THEY CAN GIVE IT TO OTHERS.

4. IF I SOW ACCORDING TO GOD'S PRINCIPLES, I WILL REAP, AND I WILL ALWAYS HAVE AN ABUNDANCE TO HELP OTHERS AS WELL AS TO MEET MY OWN NEEDS.

5. MY GIVING CAN BEGIN TO REFLECT THE RESOURCES OF MY HEAVENLY FATHER'S HOUSEHOLD, NOT MERELY MY LIMITED EARTHLY RESOURCES.

The steward who is making daily application of these five principles can live life above the circumstances. Rather than focusing on getting, one can focus on giving. Choosing to live according to these principles is the key to abundant freedom.

Because each principle is so important, let's take a careful look at them individually. Meditate on each one. Ask yourself, "How can I, as a steward, apply this principle?" Also, as you study, claim Joshua 1:8:

> This book of the law shall not depart from your mouth, but you shall meditate on it day and night, so that you may be careful to do according to all that is written in it; for then you will make your way *prosperous*, and then you will have *success* (NAS).

A SHINY STAR

Remember those days in grade school when your teacher put a big gold, red, green or silver star on your paper as a reward for your excellent work? As you apply these five principles, your life can become a "star" that radiates hope and a standard of excellence to a dark world. Your life as a steward will become a model to others.

You will note that in our discussion of these principle statements, each one is illustrated by a five-pointed star. Each point corresponds to one principle and an abbreviated version of the appropriate principle is added to the star each time it appears. As you learn and follow God's five principles of wealth distribution, you will tap His inventory and be able to live a prosperous life that is characterized by success.

PRINCIPLE 1

God, our Father, owns an infinite supply of everything that we, or anyone else, could ever need, want or desire.

That sounds nice and would, no doubt, make an excellent sermon theme. But what does this mean to you? I have turned this power-packed, formal theological statement into a short, personal sentence by writing next to the first point of the star below: My Father owns it all!

My Father owns it all.

What *does* this mean to you? Think about it—*God is the owner.* God never has and never will give up His rights of ownership. Our friend King David understood this and declared God's ownership when he proclaimed, "The earth is the Lord's, and all it contains, the world, and those who dwell in it" (Psalm 24:1, NAS).

Remember the amount given to build the temple, as recorded in 1 Chronicles 29? David and the leadership of Israel were not giving something new to God. They were simply returning to Him what was already His. As stewards they were returning well-managed investments. When the initial temple offering was collected, David exclaimed to God, "Yours is the mighty power and glory and victory and majesty. Everything in the heavens and earth is yours, O Lord, and this is your kingdom. We adore you as being in control of everything" (1 Chronicles 29:11, TLB).

Doesn't that stretch your imagination? It does mine! Our world system has subtly introduced us to the "mine and yours" way of thinking about everything. This kind of thinking is a ploy from Satan to delude our subconscious mind. As wise stewards we must reprogram the way we think about things. *Everything* belongs to our heavenly Father.

Take a moment and look around you. What do you see from where you are reading this book? Who owns all your eye can see?

According to the laws of the state of California, I own a home and two cars. I am responsible for those items legally, but are they really mine? No. My home, my cars, my clothes, the furniture in my house and the money in my bank account are not mine in the end. My Father owns it all. I am only a steward to whom God has delegated the authority to manage these possessions on His behalf.

The apostle Paul summed up God's ownership when he wrote to the Romans, "For everything comes from God alone. Everything lives by his power, and everything is for his glory. To him be glory evermore" (Romans 11:36, TLB).

God's supply is unlimited. There is absolutely no way to take anything from Him, for it's all forever in His inventory. If every one of the 4.8 billion people on earth today had all of everything they could possibly manage, we would not begin to make a dent in God's unlimited supply.

God also has the ability and authority to gather His possessions whenever He chooses. This decision rests totally in His power. In God's amazing plan, He has chosen to delegate distribution authority to His Son. In turn, His Son willfully chooses to delegate His authority to those who are called as children of God. Very simply put, *it is God to people and people to people.*

Amazing, isn't it! God has entrusted His possessions to our use. He never planned for us to be failures in managing His possessions. He expects wise management that multiplies the investment.

I'll never forget the day I turned sixteen. That was the day I obtained my driver's license. I was ready to take on the world. To demonstrate trust in me, my father and mother *chose* to allow me to have considerable use of a 1953, navy blue, four-door Chrysler sedan. Wheels! I could go where I wanted to go and do what I wanted to do. My folks chose to delegate authority to me, making me responsible for the car's upkeep and for the gas that I used. I thought of that car as "my" car.

Yet I was not the owner. The title belonged to my folks, and they could take possession of my wheels whenever they wished to do so. They continued to maintain ultimate authority over my car. As their son, I had a sense of ownership in the form of stewardship.

How do you and I as believers fit into God's plan of ownership? Remember what Jesus said just before He ascended into heaven? You can find His words in Matthew 28:18-20 (TLB):

> He told his disciples, "I have been given all authority in heaven and earth. Therefore go and make disciples in all the nations, baptizing them into the name of the Father and of

the Son and of the Holy Spirit, and then teach these new disciples to obey all the commands I have given you; and be sure of this—that I am with you always, even to the end of the world."

Jesus has been given *all* authority from God the Father. He now chooses to delegate that authority to His disciples—US. He took this action with a specific purpose in mind: so that we would carry out our assignment of making more disciples through effective stewardship. We are to take what He's given to us and use it for His purposes. We are expediters, assigned to carry out His plan. *Everything* we have is to be used to this end.

MORE THAN JUST ENOUGH

God never intended you or any other steward to have just enough to get by. He intends for you to live a life of abundance. The wealth God transfers to His kids to be distributed here on earth is but a minute part of the total wealth in His possession. God is not limited in His ability to supply abundantly.

Paul refers to God's ability to supply in Philippians 4:19 (NAS) when he writes, "And my God shall supply all your needs according to His riches in glory in Christ Jesus." Note two things: First, this is a guarantee—*He shall*; and second, God supplies *according to* His riches, not *out of* His riches. Do you understand the importance of this for us as stewards? The supply itself is an unlimited inventory. As we use what He's given to us, He has the resources to give us much more without ever diminishing His total supply! But that's only part of the story.

Paul further explains God's provision to the Corinthians in this way: And God is able to make all grace abound to you, that always having all sufficiency in everything, you may have an abundance for every good deed (2 Corinthians 9:8, NAS). God plans for you to have an abundance so you can carry out every good deed.

Although God has infinite resources, He doesn't want any waste. He therefore chooses to supply according to how His children demonstrate faithfulness in carrying out their job description through meeting the needs of others. The trustworthy steward has sufficiency in everything...yes, everything.

We all have trouble at times relating to how much is available to us. We often think of wealth in terms of supply and demand. Thus, we put greater value on items that appear to be limited in quantity rather than on those that are in great abundance. Often the value is set by our culture and our circumstances.

There seems to be an abundance of dirt on this earth. In fact, most of us try to get rid of it because we have far more around us than we need. Yet dirt becomes of great value if you have a limited supply. I am told that people moving to some South Sea coral reefs often take dirt as a part of their prized possessions so that they can enjoy living plants that only good dirt produces.

I'm afraid we often have in our possession things that are of great value to God, but due to our immaturity or lack of perspective, we fail to recognize what God has entrusted to us. I'm often reminded of Esau and Jacob, the twin sons of Isaac and Rebekah.

FOOLED

Esau was the elder son. He had a Coppertone tan complementing a body that would make any weightlifter jealous. He loved the outdoors and was a skillful hunter. Today he would no doubt serve as president of the National Wildlife Federation or in some similar position. He knew how to please his father. He never failed to bring in the best from his hunting adventures. As the firstborn, he had a definite advantage over his twin brother. He held the right to a precious inheritance that Jacob could not have.

Jacob, on the other hand, was Mr. Average. He was not a hunter and didn't seem to care much for the outdoors. He loved to manage things around home, and he loved to cook. But he was also very conniving!

Can you imagine the evening Esau returned home, exhausted and famished after a day or two of hunting? When you're tired and hungry, even stew looks like a feast. Here's what happened:

"Man, what a day! Jacob, I'm exhausted. The heat is killing me, and my feet hurt. What's for dinner? Boy am I starved! What's the red stuff there? Give me a bite."

"So you're hungry, huh, Esau? I'll make you a deal. I'll trade you a bowl of this delicious homemade stew, cornbread and honey for your birthright. How about it, brother?"

"Look, Jacob, when a guy is about to starve to death, what good is a birthright?"

"Is it a deal, then? If it is, make your vow to God that what is yours is now mine."

"O.K., Jacob, you've got a deal. I vow to God my birthright is yours in exchange for a square meal tonight. Now hurry up and get the food on the table."

Without thinking, Esau had made an unwise and immature stewardship decision. Yes, at that moment the decision seemed reasonable. He got an all-you-can-eat dinner and a drink along with it. He then went about his business as usual, never giving a thought as to what he had done. It was not until years later that he realized he had foolishly squandered the fiduciary responsibility that came with his position as the eldest son.

YOU NAME IT—HE'S GOT IT

Your heavenly Father, the great Jehovah, has an infinite supply of all you need, want or desire. He is capable and willing to give to you. He is waiting for you to write the check on His account. You need not fear that the check will bounce. The supply is far greater than your demand.

Are you aware that God's names mentioned in the Old Testament reflect His ability to supply?

> Jehovah Nissi: I am your banner.
> Jehovah Shalom: I am your peace.
> Jehovah Tsidkem: I am your righteousness.
> Jehovah Jireh: I am the one who provides.
> Jehovah Rapha: I am the one who heals.
> Jehovah Raah: I am your shepherd.
> Jehovah Shanmah: I am the one who is present.

Have you been living unwittingly on Poverty Street? Have you thought that your request might overtax God's supply? Why not decide now that you will begin to tap His infinite resources and start writing faith checks on His account? Rather than watching the parade of faithful stewards march by, you can join in and be in the parade.

God's wealth is available upon demand. All He is expecting

from you is faithfulness in the distribution of what you now have. He is ready to supply if you are ready to act, but He cannot give you more until you distribute what He's already given to you. It's up to you.

I encourage you to do the Key to Freedom, Exercise Six, before you proceed to the next chapter. By doing so, you will take the first step toward being set free to manage all that God transfers to you.

A popular chorus sums up this first principle: He's more than enough, more than enough; He is El Shaddai, the God of all plenty, the all-sufficient One, God almighty; He's more than enough for me.

Remember: *Your Father owns it all!*

KEY TO FREEDOM
Exercise Six

My Father owns it all! Sometimes it's easy to forget this important truth. To help you focus on God's ownership, spend 15 to 30 minutes listing everything you can think of that you view as being yours. Be specific. List both tangible and intangible items. Do this Exercise in the form of a written agreement with your heavenly Father.

Remember: "For everything comes from God alone. Everything lives by his power, and everything is for his glory. To Him be glory evermore" (Romans 11:36, TLB).

INVENTORY AGREEMENT BETWEEN THE STEWARD AND HIS HEAVENLY FATHER

To: My heavenly Father

From: *(name)*

Date: *(today)*

I recognize that You are the owner of EVERYTHING, God. All I have belongs to You, not to me.

As an act of gratitude for Your provisions for me, I wish to assign everything I have in my possession over to You.

Inventory List

My Father Wants Me to Give Hilariously

I'd finally done it. I had made up my mind to fall to the fad and fashion of the day in men's hairstyling. After seeing numerous ads and a number of my friends sporting the new look, I knew I had to have a perm! I called a hairdresser friend of ours, and a few days later, I left her beauty shop with the new curly style of the '80s.

Frankly, I liked the casual style. It was easy to manage, and even my friends said, "It looks so natural on you, Larry." (Little did they know that this "new look" was very similar to the photos taken of me at the 1947 Heart of America Bell dedication, when I was three years old!)

About a month after investing in my new hairstyle, an associate and I made a business trip to the Midwest. On our return to California we were to change planes in Denver, close to where my mom lives. Since I would have a two-hour layover, I called her and suggested that she come to Stapleton Airport so we could visit between planes.

As I stepped into the Denver terminal, I saw mom, her face aglow with her famous big smile. But the minute she saw me, her mouth dropped open in shock and disbelief.

Her surprised expression made me laugh. Apparently I had not told her of my hair transformation. In an instant, I knew we were in real trouble. Surrounded by hundreds of travelers in one of the most congested airports in the world, we quickly lost control of ourselves in peals of laughter.

My associate saw what was happening and decided to lose himself in the crowd to avoid being identified with this odd couple. Mom and I laughed until we cried. She laughed so hard she became quite weak, so we sat down but continued to laugh. We could not even speak. Passengers walking by assuredly thought us strange and silly.

Every time Mom thought she had regained her composure, she would look at me and burst into hilarious laughter again.

You may chuckle at this incident, but no doubt you can think of a time when you were caught up in hilarity—a time you seemed to lose control of yourself in laughter because of unexpected humorous circumstances.

PRINCIPLE 2

Have you ever thought of God caught up in hilarity? Principle #2 states: **God has an hilarious time circulating his wealth and resources and wants His children to share in this pleasure.**

I have personalized this principle by writing on the second point of the star: My Father wants me to give hilariously.

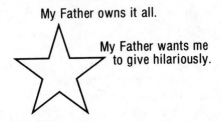

We all have a mental picture of what God does with His time. There are some who believe God spends His eternal hours wandering around a cold, stained-glass cathedral, wearing a chocolate brown monk's habit, listening to Bach, Beethoven and occasionally an angelic choir singing the Hallelujah Chorus!

Others picture Him spending countless hours at some high-tech celestial switchboard, taking hundreds of thousands of calls from His family and no doubt getting frustrated with all the pink reminder notes of requests that have to be answered.

There is no way to actually visualize how God works. Our finite minds cannot comprehend His greatness. Yet, through my study of Scripture, I have come to believe that God actively *enjoys* life. He is not a recluse. He loves His creation and His children. More than anything He wants mankind to respond willingly to His gift of love. He longs to see those who accept His Son as their Savior grow into mature believers, capable of spiritual reproduction. We please Him when we trust Him and obey Him. He has invested a lot in us. We are His inheritance. I often picture God jumping for joy when He sees His children step out in faith to carry out their responsibilities as good stewards.

To grasp the importance of this second principle, we need to better understand two words: *hilarious* and *circulation*.

As a preacher's kid, I was what you would call a regular Sunday school attender. I first enrolled at the age of three weeks and faithfully attended almost every Sunday thereafter. The theme verse for the nursery department, even though it was taken somewhat out of context, was: We shall not all sleep, but we shall all be changed.

GIVING WITH A GRIN

I started memorizing Scripture verses about the time I graduated to the mature age of three. One of the earliest verses I ever memorized was the last phrase of 2 Corinthians 9:7, "God loves a cheerful giver." For years I thought God wanted me to have a grin on my face when I put my pennies into the offering plate. The idea of being happy each time I gave money seemed logical and reasonable.

When I was five, I attended my first Billy Graham Crusade in Seattle, Washington. Cliff Barrows was in charge of taking the offering that night. He explained that giving financially should be something you wanted to do. He suggested that each person give only what he truly felt led to give. He even encouraged people to make change if they so desired as the buckets were passed.

Now that was a new twist to me—making change. The idea of making change definitely put a grin on my face. When the bucket came to me, I put in a nickel and took out a dime! Let me tell you, that was a good deal to a five-year-old!

Over the years, however, I noticed that the offering time in most churches is the low point of worship. It seems that most people have anything but a grin on their faces when the offering is taken. More often offerings remind me of a funeral. It's almost as if each person is losing his best friend (and to some, maybe that's what their money is). There is no joy, no excitement, no expression of appreciation, no laughter.

BE CHEERFUL

When someone says to you, "Be cheerful," how do you respond? If you're honest, you will admit that cheerfulness at most is a smile. When the King James translation of the Bible was completed in 1611, I'm sure 2 Corinthians 9:7 was a problem to the translators. In their Greek text they found the word *hilaros*. Because they were dealing with "holy writ," they must have decided to use a word that toned down the dynamics of what Paul was writing to the Corinthian church folk.

Hilaros is the Greek root for our English word "hilarious." A more accurate translation of the phrase found in 2 Corinthians 9:7 is: *God loves an hilarious giver.* God loves a steward who chooses to reflect God's very character. We learned in chapter 5 that our first responsibility in our job description is to "reflect God's character, love and purpose to those with whom we meet as an ambassador of His kingdom."

If God loves an hilarious giver, it stands to reason that He Himself is an hilarious giver. He wants us to follow His example. He is our model.

The word *hilaros* means "to cause to shine like the sun." Does this definition confuse you? I can understand why. It seems that the Greek definition has nothing to do with what we think of as being hilarious.

But when we think about it, it's easy to see the analogy. The sun basically has a very simple job description which God assigned to it on the day He created it: to give out heat and light. The sun was designed for a specific purpose.

We too are created with a purpose. We are created to give, just as the sun is created to give light and warmth to the earth.

It is no mistake that Paul used the word *hilaros* when writing to the Corinthians about the kind of giver God loves.

One who gives hilariously is one who gives freely as a natural response to needs and the opportunity to meet those needs. Hilarious giving is a steward's spontaneous response to do what God has called him to do. In one sense, the response is "out of control." The hilarious giver is giving from his innermost being. I can almost hear God saying, "I love the steward who freely gives in response to circumstances, just as the sun freely gives light and heat to the earth."

This principle far exceeds the giving of money, although you can easily test your hilarious giving spirit by seeing how easy or difficult it is for you to give money freely. Later we will examine 75 specific ways you can give hilariously.

Effective hilarious giving stimulates continued circulation of that which is given and always has an impact on others.

HILARITY SPREADS

Imagine yourself at a social gathering with 25 of your friends. After a period of visiting, your host announces:

"Tonight we have a game to play. The object is to lie on the floor and look at the ceiling. To be comfortable you each will need a pillow, and we have 25 ready for your use. Your pillow will be someone else's stomach! There is only one rule to the game: No matter what happens, no one is to laugh— absolutely *no laughing!*"

The events that follow the game's instructions are more fun to watch than an old "I Love Lucy" show on T.V. Once each person finds his "pillow," everyone seems to be at peace for about 20 seconds. Then dear little Susy, somewhere in the middle of the mass of bodies, looks at Joe's head of hair laying on her stomach. She thinks, *This is crazy, what if someone important walks in here and finds us all on the floor like this!*

The thought brings a smile, but then she remembers she's not to laugh. She bites her lip to suppress the chuckle. But then she notices how tense she has become. She may not be laughing on the outside, but she's dying with laughter and turmoil on the inside. Her diaphragm and stomach muscles begin to tighten and quiver.

As that happens, Joe's head, which is resting on her stomach, begins to bob up and down like an apple in a washtub at a Halloween party. Joe realizes his pillow is alive! Now he's biting *his* lip.

Susy looks down at Joe's bobbing head, and realizes she can no longer suppress the giggles. Within seconds she bursts into laughter, and in a matter of moments, her laughter has infected the whole room of people. Despite the game's rule, 25 people are now rolling on the floor in hilarious laughter.

SPONTANEOUS MULTIPLICATION

What happened at our little party game? *First,* spontaneous response resulted in hilarious giving. Susy did what any normal person in such a circumstance would do! She laughed! Although she tried desperately to suppress it, her very nature eventually forced her to burst out with laughter. She lost control. She had to laugh.

Second, hilarity spreads. In the game just played, laughter moved like a chain reaction. You can't keep a spirit of hilarity to yourself. Others around you will personally experience the results.

CIRCULATION

God's entire plan of creation is based on circulation of resources. He never intended for His stewards to use simple addition. He planned for massive multiplication. God plays a very key role in the process of circulation, but He works through a simple network: God to people; people to people.

We don't need to go far to see the greatest model of circulation ever created. Our bodies are amazing illustrations of the creative handiwork of God. Within the human body is an intricate network of muscles, organs, tissues, blood vessels, etc.—all of which are interdependent on one another. This amazing network of interdependence is a model for us in understanding how God expects us to function as believers.

God designed His creation to be a linked network; no one part is able to stand alone. He intends for this intricate network to meet every personal need of every one of us. But to do this the network must be functioning properly.

The key to successfully operating this circulation network is to use sensitive stewards who willingly and hilariously keep circulating God's wealth and resources. We are not to function under pressure of obligation. We are to be stimulated from the heart to meet the needs of others.

TWO LIMITATIONS

Are you aware that there are two limitations to hilarious giving? Paul instructs the Corinthian believers, "Let each one do just as he purposed in his heart; not grudgingly or under compulsion; for God loves a cheerful giver" (2 Corinthians 9:7, NAS).

Hilarious giving is giving because one wants to give. It cannot be done with a bad attitude. It cannot be done out of obligation. Sad to say, much of the giving done today is done under pressure. Those who feel obligated to give do not experience the joy and excitement that comes from a spirit of hilarity.

How many times have you broken down and bought a big chocolate candy bar from a child in your neighborhood who is trying to raise money for a school project? My daughters seem to get involved in such fund-raising projects every year. They go from house to house, contacting their friends and asking for participation.

Do people buy? You bet! Do people really want to buy? Not usually! Most give because of neighborhood pressure and a sense of obligation. There is little eagerness involved. One dear lady put it this way, "My doctor says I'm not to eat chocolate. I don't like those little kids coming around, but I don't want to hurt their feelings."

A few years ago an aggressive middle-aged executive trusted in Jesus Christ as his Savior and was encouraged to join a Bible study. This small group of peers helped him begin a pattern for spiritual growth. He began to blossom as he realized how much his heavenly Father had given to him.

At one of the Bible study sessions, each member of the group was asked to share an attitude change that had occurred in his life as a result of trusting Jesus Christ as personal Savior. The businessman shared:

About 18 months ago, some leaders from my church asked me to underwrite the cost of the church's new multipurpose building. They knew my family was rich materially. They explained that because my parents had been charter members in the church, they felt it would be appropriate for me to donate the funds to build the building as a memorial to my parents.

I did not want to give, but I eventually bent to the pressure I felt. I agreed to give a little over a million dollars for the building. I didn't want to; I did not feel led of God to give. But I felt it was my obligation to do so. The building is now completed and dedicated to my parents, but I've experienced no genuine joy in giving because of my attitude.

I've received a greater blessing and joy in giving my life to Jesus Christ and joining with you men to study God's Word than I felt in giving over a million dollars. I only wish I had known Jesus Christ before I was challenged to give that gift to my church. I believe if I had, I would have had quite a different reason for giving the gift.

Whether it's buying a candy bar from the neighborhood kid or giving a million dollars to your church, if it's not done with an attitude of hilarity, you cannot receive God's intended blessing.

As a junior in college, I frankly had my doubts that I had anything anyone else could benefit from having. At times I felt like a nobody with nothing to give. All I could see was my own need. I certainly was not giving hilariously!

Then, one night at a Bible study on the University of Colorado campus, I was reacquainted with a passage of Scripture that I had memorized many years earlier. I was shocked to learn that God viewed me as somebody very important. That night I personalized Ephesians 1:3-8,13-14. I got excited as I learned:

God was happy with me (verse 3).
God has blessed me (verse 3).
God gave me every spiritual blessing (verse 3).
God chose me (verse 4).
God made me holy and blameless (verse 4).
God lovingly adopted me as a son (verse 5).
This adoption is His will (verse 5).
God gave me undeserved favor (verse 6).
God freely bestowed His grace on me (verse 6).

I have been redeemed through Jesus' blood (verse 7).
I have been forgiven by God (verse 7).
God has lavished the riches of His grace upon me (verse 8).
I've been sealed in Him by the Holy Spirit (verse 13).
The Holy Spirit is God's pledge to me of my inheritance (verse 14).

That night I began to see that God had made a sacrificial investment in me. Even today I look at this list and can't help but say, "Thank You, Lord." I am an important part of God's distribution plan. You are equally important to Him. Your participation is vital to His plan.

YOU ARE SPECIAL!

You are vital because God made only one of you. You are very special to Him. Your inventory is also special—no one else has the exact inventory you have been given. The way you choose to distribute your inventory creatively to meet the needs of others will be different from the way I will distribute mine. Yet together we are a part of a worldwide service network. We are all to be wise, alert and sensitive stewards. God is holding each steward accountable for proper distribution of His inventory.

TO RECEIVE, YOU MUST GIVE

There is only one way we are able to receive more from our heavenly Father: We must give away what He's already given to us. It makes sense, doesn't it? Have you ever tried to fill a glass of water that's already full of water? You can't without first removing some of the water. As you distribute to others what God has given to you, He can refill you again to overflowing. Remember: God to people, people to people.

Why does God give you refills? Simply so that you can give even more. The more you give, the more you will receive. My heart goes out to those who hoard their time, skills and abilities, and possessions of all kinds. They are missing out on the greatest joy God has for man. Every time I hold back from giving, I miss the joy of being an Authorized Wealth Distributor for God. (We will talk more later about being an "Authorized Wealth Distributor.")

Do you see now why Paul quoted Jesus in Acts 20:35, "It is

more blessed to give than to receive"? Hilarity comes through giving. It's fun. It's exciting. It's living on the edge of faith. It's trusting Him to supply. It's getting a taste of what is to come.

This process of distribution was modeled to us by Jesus Himself. He gave His life so that He would receive us as adopted children. We now can give so that we can receive a multiplied return—*not to keep this return, but to give it away again.* "He made Him who knew no sin to be sin on our behalf, that we might become the righteousness of God in Him" (2 Corinthians 5:21, NAS).

The one who chooses to hoard will eventually lose what he has hoarded. The one who chooses to give will gain. "For whoever wishes to save his life shall lose it; but whoever loses his life for My sake shall find it" (Matthew 16:25, NAS).

Jesus so simply summarized the results of giving: "Give, and it will be given to you; good measure, pressed down, shaken together, running over, they will pour into your lap. For by your standard of measure it will be measured to you in return" (Luke 6:38, NAS).

When I look at this verse, I think of an overflowing triple-dipper, old-fashioned, handpacked ice cream cone. Imagine your three favorite flavors piled high on a cone just waiting to satisfy your taste buds. Every lick is heavenly. Why? Because it's been distributed in good measure, pressed down, shaken together and running over. There's no fluff, no fillers, no air. It's concentrated, genuine, packed and filling.

As we give hilariously, Jesus promises that the return we can expect will be rich, full, complete, filling—and more than we could ever imagine to be adequate.

DISTRIBUTION PRIORITIES

Your highest priority as a steward is to ensure that network distribution is occurring. You are representing the greatest wealth distributor of all time; therefore, everything you do should be a reflection of His plan of circulation. You accomplish this priority in three ways:

1. *Personally giving.* You have the privilege of being a model. People around you need to see an Authorized Wealth Distributor

in action, for your actions will speak far more loudly than your words. The way in which you hilariously circulate what you have in your inventory will be a testimony to others.

You have countless items in your inventory that you can distribute. You have material possessions, of course, but as we will see in chapter 12, these are only a small part of the many gifts you have to give.

2. *Stimulating others to give.* Not only are you to give, but you are also to help others see that they too have much to give. Every person alive has exactly what someone else needs.

My good friend Jim Jackson of Evergreen, Colorado, has developed a dynamic stewardship course that he calls "Christianomics." Throughout the text and study, he helps others face themselves and deal with the question of the ages: What'cha gonna do with what'cha got?

One of the most exciting concepts he has developed is a simple, yet creative, way to help the steward give, as well as to stimulate the receiver to give. He teaches the student of Christianomics that God has given him a "trust account" to manage. The student does this by distributing what God has given him to others. When a steward distributes something from his inventory to another person, this is called a "Trust Account Transfer"(TAT). That student is to give a TAT slip (that looks like a banking check) to the other person as he distributes his managed inventory. Through this method, the receiver gets the picture that what has been received can also be redistributed to others. The TAT slips help stimulate an active network distribution.

3. *Graciously receiving from others.* One of the saddest things I've observed over the years is people refusing someone else's desire to give to them. I'm sure you've witnessed restaurant scenes like this one:

> Two couples are out to dinner. They enjoy each other's company— until the waitress brings the bill, when each man decides he is going to pay for the meal. As they argue over who gets the check, their happy fellowship sours and becomes an emotional dogfight. Finally the waitress must split the check just to restore peace

Such an incident can be avoided if we are willing to receive as well as give.

When someone initiates giving to you, be gracious and warmly receive the gift. Giving to you is likely that person's way of participating in hilarious giving. Remember: God to people; people to people.

After you have received, you will have numerous opportunities to multiply that which you have received. God will continue to add to your inventory as you are distributing what He's already given to you. Don't be concerned that you must pay back someone for a gift of time, talent or possessions given to you.

You should not be concerned with direct return. God may allow you to give to that person when he has a need at a later time. On the other hand, God may intend for you to give to meet another's need. Circulating God's wealth and resources can create a network of giving. Properly functioning, everyone—Christian and non-Christian alike—will feel the impact of the distribution system.

As I receive from others, I continually pray, "Lord, I've received from Your circulation network. Now make me sensitive to others: What have You given to me that I am to give to someone else now? What do You want me to give that will keep Your wealth and resources in constant circulation?"

GOD'S VIEW OF HILARIOUS GIVING

The two most dynamic chapters in Scripture concerning God's view on giving and receiving are found in 2 Corinthians 8 and 9. Paul's purpose for writing was to encourage a financial collection of funds for a pledge fulfillment that the believers in Corinth had previously made. Although the specific subject deals with giving money, I believe we can learn a good deal about giving freely from all that we receive from our Father.

Chapter 8 is loaded with nuggets on hilarious giving. As we look at this chapter, ask God to give you understanding so that you can begin to apply what you read.

Paul writes:

> Now I want to tell you what God in his grace has done for the churches in Macedonia (2 Corinthians 8:1, TLB).

Truth:

HILARIOUS GIVING COMES FROM GOD.
HILARIOUS GIVING DEMANDS THAT ONE MUST FIRST
RECEIVE FROM GOD.
HILARIOUS GIVING CIRCULATES GOD'S UNDE-
SERVED FAVOR.

☆ ☆ ☆

Though they have been going through much trouble and hard
times, they have mixed their wonderful joy with their deep
poverty, and the result has been an overflow of giving to
others (2 Corinthians 8:2, TLB).

Truth:

HILARIOUS GIVING STARTS WITH AN ATTITUDE.
HILARIOUS GIVING STIMULATES AN ABUNDANCE OF
JOY.
WHAT ONE GIVES OR HOW MUCH ONE GIVES IS NOT
THE ISSUE.
THE ATTITUDE IN GIVING MAKES ALL THE DIFFER-
ENCE IN THE WORLD.

☆ ☆ ☆

They gave not only what they could afford, but far more; and
I can testify that they did it because they wanted to, and not
because of nagging on my part (2 Corinthians 8:3, TLB).

Truth:

HILARIOUS GIVING IS FREE FROM PRESSURE OR
COERCION.
HILARIOUS GIVING IS GIVING BECAUSE YOU WANT
TO, NOT BECAUSE YOU HAVE TO.

☆ ☆ ☆

They begged us to take the money so they could share in the
joy of helping the Christians in Jerusalem (2 Corinthians 8:4,
TLB).

Truth:

HILARIOUS GIVING IS A PRIVILEGE WHICH RESULTS
IN A BOND OF UNITY AMONG BELIEVERS.

☆ ☆ ☆

Best of all, they went beyond our highest hopes, for their first
action was to dedicate themselves to the Lord and to us, for

whatever directions God might give to them through us (2 Corinthians 8:5, TLB).

Truth:

HILARIOUS GIVING BEGINS BY GIVING YOURSELF TO THE LORD.
HILARIOUS GIVING EXCEEDS MAN'S EXPECTATIONS.
HILARIOUS GIVING SEEKS GOD'S DIRECTION.
HILARIOUS GIVING RESPONDS TO THE NEEDS OF OTHERS.

☆   ☆   ☆

They were so enthusiastic about it that we have urged Titus, who encouraged your giving in the first place, to visit you and encourage you to complete your share in this ministry of giving (2 Corinthians 8:6, TLB).

Truth:

HILARIOUS GIVING IS ENTHUSIASTIC.
HILARIOUS GIVING IS STIMULATED BY CHRISTIAN LEADERSHIP.
HILARIOUS GIVING IS MINISTRY IN ACTION.

☆   ☆   ☆

You people there are leaders in so many ways—you have so much faith, so many good preachers, so much learning, so much enthusiasm, so much love for us. Now I want you to be leaders also in the spirit of cheerful giving (2 Corinthians 8:7, TLB).

Truth:

HILARIOUS GIVING IS AN ACT OF THE WILL.
HILARIOUS GIVING IS THE MARK OF MATURING BE-LIEVERS.
HILARIOUS GIVING STIMULATES OTHERS TO GIVE.

☆   ☆   ☆

I am not giving you an order; I am not saying you must do it, but others are eager for it. This is one way to prove that your love is real, that it goes beyond mere words (2 Corinthians 8:8, TLB).

Truth:

HILARIOUS GIVING CANNOT OCCUR WHEN THE GIVER IS UNDER PRESSURE TO GIVE.

HILARIOUS GIVING IS PROOF THAT CHRISTIAN LOVE
IS REAL.
HILARIOUS GIVING IS LOVE IN ACTION.

☆ ☆ ☆

You know how full of love and kindness our Lord Jesus was:
though he was so very rich, yet to help you he became so very
poor, so that by being poor he could make you rich (2 Corinthians 8:9, TLB).

Truth:

HILARIOUS GIVING WAS MODELED FOR US BY THE
LORD JESUS.
HILARIOUS GIVING CONSIDERS ANOTHER'S NEEDS A
PRIORITY.
HILARIOUS GIVING PRODUCES RESULTS.

☆ ☆ ☆

Having started the ball rolling so enthusiastically, you should
carry this project through to completion just as gladly, giving
whatever you can out of whatever you have. Let your enthusiastic idea at the start be equalled by your realistic action
now (2 Corinthians 8:11, TLB).

Truth:

HILARIOUS GIVING CAN BE INTERRUPTED BY THE
THINGS OF THE WORLD.
HILARIOUS GIVING RELIES ON DECISIVE ACTION OF
THE GIVER.

☆ ☆ ☆

If you are really eager to give, then it isn't important how
much you have to give. God wants you to give what you have,
not what you haven't (2 Corinthians 8:12, TLB).

Truth:

HILARIOUS GIVING DOES NOT RELY ON QUANTITY
TO GIVE.
HILARIOUS GIVING COMES FROM WHAT ONE HAS,
NOT WHAT ONE DOESN'T HAVE.

☆ ☆ ☆

Did Mrs. Weber see a return on her investment of a letter?
Yes! Letters came in by the thousands; each told its own story
and enclosed in each was at least a penny. As a bonus Mrs. Weber

was blessed by seeing the Heart of America Bell become a reality on Thanksgiving Day, 1947.

Are you ready to be used by God as an hilarious giver? I know that God is ready. He's waiting for your availability. He wants you involved in His distribution network. Go for it!

Before moving on to chapter 8, I encourage you to spend 10 to 15 minutes working on your Key to Freedom, Exercise Seven.

Remember: God to people; people to people. *God wants you to give hilariously!*

KEY TO FREEDOM
Exercise Seven

You probably have experienced giving under pressure. Jot down three different occasions when you gave your time, talent or treasure but were not excited about doing so. How did you really feel on those occasions?

1.

2.

3.

In what practical ways can you begin to give hilariously?

What are some ways you can stimulate others to give hilariously?

Chapter **8**

My Father Wants Me to Ask

After a 22-hour drive from Colorado to California in early June, 1969, I finally arrived at my destination—beautiful Arrowhead Springs, the International Headquarters of Campus Crusade for Christ.

Nine months earlier, I had left Arrowhead Springs in my trusty Oldsmobile Cutlass. The two of us had a special mission—we traveled together through 31 states and logged over 35,000 miles as I set up college concerts for the New Folk, an evangelistic music group.

It felt good to be home at last. Nine months alone on the road can drain anyone. I was looking forward eagerly to living in my own apartment for the summer, sleeping in the same bed for three months, renewing old friendships, and having a few dates like a normal person.

Soon after I arrived I headed for the president's office, hoping to find a gal from the East Coast who was assigned to work there temporarily. Maybe she would like to go out for coffee.

She wasn't in. Only the full-time secretary for the office was there—a cute girl named Pat Menghini, whom I immediately recognized from the summer before. I had tried to get to know her then, but she was "booked." I never made it to first base.

In the office we exchanged friendly greetings for a few moments. I was about to be late for another appointment, so I excused myself. But as I left I made a mental note that Pat was still around. Perhaps she might have some time for me *this* summer.

It wasn't long before we had our first date, when I asked Pat to join me for the day at an amusement park. She accepted, and I was ecstatic!

We were on Tom Sawyer Island when it happened. Somehow I had to take her hand to steady her, but we never let go! I liked her laugh, her personality, her way of doing things; something was happening...she was special.

The more we spent time together the next couple of weeks, the more we knew there was a special dimension to our relationship. I knew this was God's choice for my mate. I sensed she felt the same way.

HAVE YOU ASKED?

My summer assignment at Arrowhead Springs was briefly interrupted with a four-day trip to Colorado for a family reunion. One afternoon I confided in my brother, "Jerry, I'm going to marry a girl I met about a month ago. She's a wonderful Christian and is excited about serving the Lord. We really fit. She's the one."

Jerry had a simple but very direct question, "Have you asked her to marry you?"

"No, Jerry..."

"Well, you will never marry her unless you ask her to marry you." That was the end of the conversation.

Jerry was more right than I wanted my brother to be. For Pat to marry me, I had to ask her to do so.

Three days later when Pat picked me up at the airport, she was as beautiful as ever. I had really missed her in those four days away. She seemed to have missed me, too.

That night, with my faithful trusty Cutlass as my witness, I asked Pat to be my wife. Her response hit me between the eyes, "You know I will; I love you, Larry."

Because I asked Pat to marry me on August 18, 1969, we now have spent a good number of wonderful years together. She's my dearest friend, best counsel, greatest lover, a wise confidante and my favorite companion. To receive all of this and more, all I had to do was ask.

Pennies came from across America in 1947 to help a little country church get a bell because Mrs. Weber *asked* Uncle Ben for a bell for the church. If Mrs. Weber had not asked, the Heart's Desire radio team would never have learned of the need, and they in turn would not have asked Americans to send their pennies. To receive, one must ask.

PRINCIPLE 3

It pleases God when His children ask for, then diligently seek, some of their inheritance so they can give it to others.

Put more simply, this third principle becomes: My Father wants me to ask.

My Father owns it all.

My Father wants me to give hilariously.

My Father wants me to ask.

I've observed that most people view asking as hurting someone, rather than helping them. Have you ever felt this way?

Asking someone to do something is the greatest way to demonstrate confidence in that person. Asking should be the natural result of a developing relationship. God wants us to ask. He desires that we express our concerns, needs, wants and desires to Him. He wants our requests to be the overflow of our relationship with Him.

Look at a few of the choice promises we find from our heavenly Father:

> You can get anything—ANYTHING you ask for in prayer—if you believe (Matthew 21:22, TLB).

> In solemn truth I tell you, anyone believing in me shall do the same miracles I have done, and even greater ones, because I am going to be with the Father. You can ask him for ANYTHING, using my name, and I will do it, for this will bring praise to the Father because of what I, the Son, will do for

you. Yes, ask ANYTHING, using my name, and I will do it
(John 14:12-14, TLB).

But if you stay in me and obey my commands, you may ask
any request you like, and it will be granted (John 15:7, TLB).

You haven't tried this before, [but begin now]. Ask, using my
name, and you will receive, and your cup of joy will overflow
(John 16:24, TLB).

I don't know about you, but I get the feeling from reading
these nuggets that the Lord Jesus expects us to be telling Him
what's on our hearts. He is ready to hear and to respond to our
requests.

Missionary Jim Elliott painted a graphic word picture when
he wrote in his diary, "God is on His throne, and we are on His
footstool—and we are only a knee away."

RELATIONSHIP

Is your relationship with God so close that you feel you're at
His footstool, that you are free to express to Him all that's on
your heart? He wants open communication with each of His stewards. He's waiting to hear you ask so that He can respond to your
request.

God's Word is full of classic testimonies of men whose relationship with God allowed them to experience the power of God. He
was an abundant supplier in response to the needs that faced them:

Because of Noah's relationship with God, he received the grace
of God. God entrusted to him the blueprint for a seagoing vessel
that saved Noah's family from the flood. Noah faithfully took the
steps necessary to construct a ship 450 feet long, 75 feet wide and
45 feet high, in the middle of dry, desert ground. He gave to his
sons what God gave to him. As a result, the animals of the earth
and Noah's entire family were saved so that they could give again
to a new generation.

Because of Moses' relationship with God, an entire nation was
set free from bondage. Moses' relationship with God was so honest
that he even asked God to send another leader. God, however,
chose Moses to be His chief steward—the man to give leadership
to the Exodus. God did answer his request by providing Aaron to
speak for Moses. Moses gave as God instructed.

Because of Gideon's relationship with God, he could ask God to confirm His will when Gideon put out a fleece. Gideon then accepted God's direction and was appointed to give leadership to three hundred chosen men. Because of Gideon's obedience and faithfulness as a steward, the entire Midianite army was defeated.

Because of Daniel's relationship with God, he was chosen to serve as counselor to King Nebuchadnezzar. When the king awoke with a terrifying nightmare one night, he summoned his wisest men to tell him the meaning of his dream. Daniel and his three friends—Shadrach, Meshach and Abednego—all went to prayer, asking God to show them the secret of the dream. God responded to the request and gave Daniel the interpretation. While serving later under King Darius, Daniel was thrown into the lions' den because he refused to obey a law of the Medes and Persians—forbidding anyone in the kingdom to ask a favor of God or any man except the king himself. Daniel was thrown to the lions for one reason: He continued to pray to his God three times a day. God sent His angel to shut the lions' mouths because Daniel was demonstrating obedient stewardship by asking God for direction.

Because of Elijah's relationship with God, he was able to take on King Ahab and Queen Jezebel's sinful kingdom. On Mount Carmel, Elijah challenged the king and queen and their 450 pagan Baal prophets to a contest to determine the true God. After the prophets of Baal spent the entire day dancing, shouting and cutting their bodies, trying to get Baal's attention to come and light the fire to the prepared sacrifice, they gave up. Elijah then laid out his sacrifice and to make it harder, poured five barrels of water on the altar. Then he prayed, "O Lord God of Abraham, Isaac and Israel, prove today that you are the God of Israel and that I am your servant; prove that I have done all this at your command. O Lord, answer me! Answer me so these people will know that you are God and that you have brought them back to yourself." (1 Kings 18:36, TLB). Fire flashed from heaven, totally consuming the waterlogged sacrifice. Elijah asked, and God answered.

Because of David's relationship with God, he had confidence to act with boldness in circumstances which would overwhelm most people. When David went to battle against nine-foot Goliath, he shouted to the giant, "You come to me with sword and spear, but I come to you in the name of the Lord....and Israel will learn that the Lord does not depend on weapons to fulfill his plans—he works without regard to human means! He will give you to us!" (1 Samuel 17:45, 47, TLB). David's confidence was based on his belief that God would answer his requests.

Because of Solomon's relationship with God, he reigned as king of Israel for forty years. As Solomon took the throne, God said to him, "Ask me for anything, and I will give it to you!" Solomon, as you know, asked God to give him wisdom and knowledge to rule his people properly. Then God replied, "Because your greatest desire is to help your people, and you haven't asked for personal wealth and honor, and you haven't asked me to curse your enemies, and you haven't asked for a long life, but for wisdom and knowledge to properly guide my people—yes, I am giving you the wisdom and knowledge you asked for! And I am also giving you such riches, wealth and honor as no other king has ever had before you!" (2 Chronicles 1:7-12, TLB). Solomon was given an abundance because he asked God for what was really important.

What comes to your mind when you are confronted with these heroes of the faith? I used to get a little frustrated as I read accounts of the outstanding men God chose to lead His people. I thought, *God, that's great, but these men seem to be outstanding leaders. How about the average people—the ones who never make the front page—the ones like me*?

JUST AN ORDINARY MAN

God answered my question a few years ago by introducing me to an ordinary man. I met him in 1 Chronicles 4:9,10. Jabez was a guy like you and me. In fact, the meaning of his name gives you an idea of how typical he is to most of us who stand in awe of such spiritual giants as Daniel, David and Solomon. Jabez means "distress." His mother gave him this name because of the difficult labor that she experienced at the time of his birth.

For years I missed hearing about Jabez. His name is mentioned in only one place in Scripture—in the middle of one of those dynamic "begot" sections!

Then I was introduced to Jabez through a speaker who challenged me to pray the prayer that Jabez prayed. He prayed, "Oh that Thou wouldst bless me indeed, and enlarge my border, and that Thy hand might be with me, and that Thou wouldst keep me from harm, that it may not pain me" (1 Chronicles 4:10, NAS).

Do you know how God responded to Jabez's request? Scripture says, "And God granted him what he requested" (1 Chronicles 4:10, NAS). How simple. How powerful. His four-part request was graciously received by God, and He did exactly what Jabez requested:

1. God's blessing poured out upon him.

2. God enlarged his border. No doubt this included the size of his land holdings, but very likely it also included his influence and perspective as well.

3. God kept His hand on him. There is no better protection in a world of evil.

4. God kept Satan from him. With God's hand on his shoulder, Jabez experienced freedom from the power of sin.

Just think of it, an ordinary guy receiving all of this just because he asked! Probably no other prayer in Scripture has impacted my life as this one has. I have claimed this as my life prayer, and I have already seen God respond just as He responded to ordinary Jabez over three thousand years ago.

UNLOCKING YOUR LIMITATIONS

Probably nothing pleases God more than hearing His children ask Him for wisdom, direction, understanding and other needs. Asking God for what you see as your need demonstrates to Him that you recognize His leadership and lordship. You demonstrate dependence on Him and confidence in Him when you ask for His divine intervention.

When you ask you should be honest, transparent and regular. There is no need to play games with God. He already knows your heart. Remember, seeking Him for counsel and direction is not merely an activity. Asking Him is a testimony of your relationship with Him.

A few years ago at a conference, I was privileged to sit under the teaching of Dr. Jack Taylor. His insight into asking God made the profound so simple. He suggested that the key which unlocks the treasures of God's inventory to us, His children, is found in 1 John 5:14,15 (NAS):

> And this is the confidence which we have before Him, that, if we ask anything according to His will, He hears us. And if we know that He hears us in whatever we ask, we know that we have the requests which we have asked from Him.

Read the verse again. What do you see? I'm afraid to most people these are just nice words. But these two little verses can strip away your limitations if you choose to *act* on their promise.

Do you have confidence that God can do anything? I'm afraid that all too often we act as if God were limited in His ability to respond to our requests. Or we may view God as sitting at His computer, calling up our past failures to see if we deserve our current requests. But God does not keep a tally of our past sins. When He forgives us, He *removes* our shortcomings and sin from His memory bank and remembers them against us no more. All He needs from us is our confidence in Him to act.

The size of the request does not bother Him. He is capable of responding to a giant request just as easily as to a tiny one. So why ask for peanuts when God can give you a seven-course meal? He has absolutely no reason to withhold anything from His children, unless it is truly harmful to us.

Do you have confidence that if you ask according to His will, He hears? Many times we have a tendency to think, *He's too busy to take my request*, or *I don't want to bother Him with such a petty problem*. There's good news! God hears! He's not preoccupied with heavenly activity. If you ask according to His will, He hears. It's that simple.

Do you have confidence that when He hears you, and you confess that He hears you and believe this, then He will grant your request of Him? If you have confidence in God, you need to demonstrate your faith in Him by acting as if it is so when it isn't so, so it *will* be so.

When you come right down to the bottom line, the issue is not a matter of God answering, but of your having *confidence* in Him to answer. If you have confidence, why not ask and then begin telling others that God *has* answered your request? Begin thanking Him for the answer and praising Him for His response. True, you may not have the tangible results of the answer in hand, but that need not stop you from demonstrating your confidence in God by faith. Are you going to trust God by faith, or are you going to trust in some tangible result?

Do you have confidence in God's faithfulness? No doubt you have experienced a time delay in seeing the tangible result of your prayer to God. The reason we experience such apparent delays is not that God hasn't answered. It is that, from our limited perspective, our needs must be met within a particular time frame. But remember this: God always delivers on time—not one second too early or one second too late.

GOD IS NOT ON VACATION!

Have you ever asked God for something, yet felt that He ignored your request? I'm sure we've all experienced the time delay crisis. But this delay in no way implies that God is on vacation or is ignoring you.

Delays in delivery are in your best interest. God knows the best timing for you. Even when things might look hopeless to you, God sees things differently and knows just the right timing.

Parents experience this with their children. A few years ago, my younger daughter, Jessica, came to me and asked me to allow her to ride her bicycle in the street in front of our home. At the time she was five years old. She still had training wheels on her bicycle.

"Can you ride your bike without the training wheels, Jessica? I want you to be able to ride in the street, too; but in order for me to say yes, I need to see how well you can ride without the training wheels."

Jessica responded, "Oh sure, Dad, that's easy." So I removed the training wheels, and she confidently got on her bike. But she had ridden only one foot when she fell. Even my help didn't seem to benefit her much that day. She just couldn't get the hang of steering, peddling and balancing herself all at the same time.

After an hour of watching her do her best to ride without the training wheels, I decided she wasn't ready for the street. I did not tell her she could *never* ride in the street; however, I did explain that before she went into the street, she first had to conquer the two wheels on the sidewalk. I wanted to deliver her request; but because of her lack of maturity and ability, she would have to wait.

Two years passed, and Jessica was still riding on the sidewalk with the training wheels. She occasionally asked me about the street, but I reminded her what had to happen first. There were times when the two of us would go for a checkout, but each time she proved not to be ready.

On Easter Sunday, when Jessica was seven, she came to me and said, "Dad, let's go take off my training wheels. I'm ready to ride my bike without them."

We took the bike to a park area near our home. I gave her a good push, and she was off. First ten feet, then twenty-five feet, then fifty feet, then half a block. Within thirty minutes, she was riding very well on a nearby school playground. She was ready for new challenges.

Today Jessica can ride in the street with supervision. There will come a time when I will be able to trust her to ride alone to a friend's house, but that is in the future. I have not changed in my commitment to let her ride in the street. Jessica has changed. She has balance, she's learning bike safety rules and she's increasing daily in her ability to assume responsibility.

I see God responding to us much as I had to respond to Jessica. Just as it took two years for her to be ready to receive her request, so it often takes us time to grow spiritually before God is able to deliver our request to us. He knows when we are ready to handle what we have asked for.

During the two-year bike-riding process, Jessica never complained about not riding in the street—even though she asked often and even though her older sister, Cari, had permission to ride in the street. Jessica understood that my response was not based on my ability but on hers.

As you grow in your walk of faith, God does not mind your asking as often as you want. Be persistent. In the process of asking, you no doubt will learn much about yourself and, I hope, much about your heavenly Father. Keep in mind, however, that your persistent asking is of greater benefit to you than it is to Him.

He has already answered your request and will not fail to deliver it at just the right time.

The next time you find yourself repeating the same request, don't plead or beg. Rather, ask God to allow you to grow and mature as you wait for the arrival of His timed delivery.

We are very limited in our perspective of things. We don't see things as God does. If He were to act and deliver on our demand, He would not be stimulating our spiritual growth. It is important, therefore, that we maintain an attitude of gratitude.

We must continue to express gratitude to God for His wisdom, understanding, insight and concern for our best interest. Thanking Him continually frees our spirit to learn from our times of waiting. Let praise be on your lips at all times; despite the circumstances, give praise and thanksgiving to Him.

Don't allow the spirit of ingratitude to creep in like a thief in the night. The side effects of ingratitude are painful. Ingratitude leads to poor health, a loss of hope, a bitter spirit, depression and negative thoughts. Social relationships crumble, and soon irresponsibility becomes the hallmark of one's life. Greed and selfishness eat away at the soul.

Paul summed up the bitter results of a spirit of ingratitude:

> For even though they knew God, they did not honor Him as God, or give thanks; but they become futile in their speculations, and their foolish heart was darkened (Romans 1:21, NAS).

There are times when you need to be still and let God speak to you. I'm sure there are many times God wants to answer you, but He has to wait for you to stop running or talking. He will wait until you are ready to listen.

As you ask from God, don't forget why He wants you to ask. He wants to give to you so that you can give to others. Whatever you ask of God should be something that can in some way be given to someone else. Whatever God gives to you becomes a part of your working inventory as a steward. What you ask for and then receive may change form before it is passed on to benefit someone else, but it is to be used to meet someone else's need as well as yours.

Keep in mind also that God will use you as a steward to make deliveries for Him. Wouldn't it be embarrassing to learn that a friend's request never got answered because you failed to make a Spirit-directed transfer from your inventory to his (so someone else received that pleasure)?

EXPRESS THANKS

There are so many ways to say thanks to God for providing for us. Be creative in expressing thanks. Do things that cause you to focus on all that He's done for you. One wonderful way to say thanks to God is through generous financial giving to His work around the world.

Remember: Your Father wants you to ask.

KEY TO FREEDOM
Exercise Eight

1 John 5:14,15 (NAS) says:

> And this is the confidence which we have before Him, that, if we ask anything according to His will, He hears us. And if we know that He hears us in whatever we ask, we know that we have the requests which we have asked from Him.

Based on this promise, write a prayer to your heavenly Father, asking Him for something that is on your heart. Close your written prayer with thanksgiving and confidence in Him and His timing.

My prayer:

This prayer is submitted on _____,
                                        (date)

by_____.
          (signature)

From now on you need not ask for this request again, based on 1 John 5:14,15. But you are free to "remind" Him of the request as often as you want. Whenever you mention this request to God, remember to thank Him that your answer is on the way and that you are choosing to trust Him, rather than trusting your circumstances.

Chapter 9

What I Sow, I Will Reap

One Saturday morning in early April, Pat and I decided to go for it; we would plant a home garden.

Raised in western Colorado, I was very familiar with the gardening process. Relatives and church members from Dad's little church were always eager to provide us with sacks of their fresh garden vegetables. Every sack was a tribute to their labors as well as to the law of the harvest.

Nothing whets my palate more than fresh garden and orchard produce. Childhood summers were filled with fresh green beans, beets, sweet corn, peas, carrots, peaches, pears, plums, apricots, grapes, and myriad other mouth-watering delights. With those memories in mind, and with all of my second-hand knowledge of farming and harvesting, I thought planting a backyard garden would be simple enough. I recognized the principle: Whatever a man sows, this he will reap. There was no reason, I figured, that I should not expect an abundant harvest.

While the sun was still low in the eastern sky, I headed for the backyard with my garden tools. I felt like a pioneer about to conquer the great frontier! Because my backyard had never had a garden plot, I had to start by digging out the grass—not a very time-consuming task, or so I thought!

But as the sun was sinking in the West many hours later, I finally cleared out the last of the creeping grass roots. What I had anticipated would take only a few hours took an entire day.

My hands were sore; my back ached; I was sunburned; I was exhausted. As I climbed into bed that night, I thought to myself, *Is this going to be worth it?*

I continued to prepare the ground, adding fertilizer and other minerals to the soil. At last I was ready to plant. I followed the instructions on each package of seeds—that is, to a point. On a few packages the instructions were specific: when the little shoots sprouted, I was to thin the plants by pulling some of them out.

Here I rebelled. No way was I going to throw away the little seedlings. After all, I wanted a big crop. It simply did not make sense to me to pull up half of the garden! Without further counsel, I decided not to thin the seedlings. As things began to grow, Pat and I grew excited about the approaching harvest time.

Then we had a hot spell. Despite my watering, the heat began to hurt the crops. The lettuce wilted long before the season was over. The peas and beans died on the vine. I never even saw a beet. The sweet corn? Beautiful plants but no ears of corn. As for the tomatoes, the blossoms wouldn't even set.

And the carrots? I got carrots all right, but because I had refused to thin them, they were the scrawniest things I'd ever seen! The one redeeming crop was our zucchini and crookneck squash.

As the summer wore on and the heat soared to over 100 degrees for days at a time, I decided that city farming was not worth my effort. No matter what I tried, I was unable to redeem anything but the squash. But I learned through my gardening experience that there is both a principle and a procedure if one wants to experience an abundant harvest.

PRINCIPLE 4

If I sow according to God's principles, I will reap, and I will always have an abundance to help others as well as to meet my own needs.

To put it in simple personal terms: What I sow, I will reap.

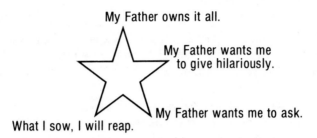

My Father owns it all.

My Father wants me to give hilariously.

My Father wants me to ask.

What I sow, I will reap.

To see the practical reality of this principle work in your life, you need to recognize certain conditions which govern a bountiful harvest.

As I look back to my gardening venture, I realize now that although I followed *some* of the procedures listed in the instructions, I also took the liberty to ignore some of the others and do as I pleased. Do you know what my two main problems were? My selfishness and my greed!

For example, the instructions said to thin; I said, "No way!" The instructions said not to plant after a certain time of year (due to California heat). I went ahead and planted anyway. I was advised to water my garden in the evening or early morning; I chose to do it when it was convenient—occasionally forgetting to water at all.

I planted a garden, but I failed to tend to my garden according to wise counsel. I did enough of the right things to give the appearance of a potential harvest, but I fell short. I failed to recognize that you have to obey certain farming principles in order to be successful.

On the other hand, a friend of mine has the proverbial green thumb. Anything he plants grows. Consequently, he is able to enjoy home-grown fruit, fresh garden veggies and beautiful flowers almost year-round. Because he has learned to operate according to the laws of the harvest, the result is a bountiful yield.

As I've compared my garden failure to successful farming endeavors, I've come up with six critical elements that are necessary to produce a bountiful harvest. I believe these six elements relate not only to farming, but also to the very heart of stewardship and to our fourth principle.

1. *Focus on the harvest.* I've never met a farmer yet who worked for months only to say, "I wasn't expecting a harvest—that was only for fun. I only wanted to work the process." A farmer plants in anticipation of how much he expects to reap at harvest time.

Likewise, you should know what to expect as a result of your labor. Keep a mental picture in your mind of what you will actually see at the end of the process.

Each of us determines how much God will be able to bless us. If you want a little, give a little. If you want a lot, give a lot. God uses what we sow to provide our return on the harvest. Although we are to focus on the harvest, Jesus admonishes us not to worry about the return:

> Don't worry about THINGS—food, drink, and clothes. For you already have life and a body—and they are far more important than what to eat and wear. Look at the birds! They don't worry about what to eat—they don't need to sow or reap or store up food—for your heavenly Father feeds them. And you are far more valuable to him than they are (Matthew 6:25,26, TLB).

Jesus promises to be our total sufficiency. Our responsibility is to manage wisely, plan toward the return and allow Him to produce the harvest.

2. *Remain committed to the end.* The farmer knows that planting is only a first step toward harvest. He must be committed to following through on the entire process. To obtain the expected results takes additional time, talent and treasure.

No farmer in his right mind would decide to take a four-week vacation during the growing months of his crops. Similarly, you must not change direction halfway through a time of spiritual growth if you wish to have a maximum return on your investment.

3. *Sow the right seed with generosity.* The farmer who properly plants corn, expects corn. If he properly plants a crop of grain, he expects a harvest of grain. That which is planted is the basis of the return.

In Genesis, God gives specific instructions to the seed-bearing plants:

> Let the earth burst forth with every sort of grass and seed-bearing plant, and fruit trees with seeds inside the fruit, *so that* these seeds will produce the kinds of plants and fruits they come from (Genesis 1:11, TLB).

Around forty years ago, the former owner of our home planted an avocado tree in the backyard. What started out as a little tree now stretches over fifty feet into the California sky. This mature tree faithfully produces one avocado crop each year. I've never found an apple hanging from its branches. God made that tree to produce only one type of fruit—avocados.

If you sow a seed of love, expect a harvest of love. If you sow a seed of joy, peace or concern, expect a multiplied harvest of the seed sown. If you sow money, what can you expect to receive in return? According to the law of the harvest, you can expect to receive money.

Keep in mind that God controls the time and quantity of the return. You cannot play games with His harvest or manipulate Him into creating a return so that you can hoard. What you sow, God returns to you in overflowing measure so that you can give far more. The more you receive, the more you are to give.

Doesn't it stand to reason that we should sow with generosity? A wise farmer is never stingy with his seed. He knows he must give away his seed in order for it to produce an anticipated harvest. The more generously you sow, the more bountiful will be your harvest.

A word of caution: The principle of sowing and reaping is not limited only to positive, good things that can be planted. Be careful not to sow discord, hate, bickering, grumbling, criticism, gossip, and other seeds of division and discontent. God's Word warns us:

> Do not be deceived, God is not mocked; for whatever a man sows, this he will also reap. For the one who sows to his own flesh shall from the flesh reap corruption, but the one who sows to the Spirit shall from the Spirit reap eternal life (Galatians 6:7,8, NAS).

During my time on the staff of Campus Crusade for Christ,

I came to deeply appreciate president Bill Bright's example and insight on living the Christian life in the power of the Holy Spirit. He is especially concerned about believers who do not take their stewardship responsibilities seriously. Dr. Bright once stated:

> I am amazed at the life-style of the average Christian, a life-style that differs little from that of nonbelievers in terms of attitudes, actions, motives, desires and words. Many Christians are experiencing financial difficulty, emotional turmoil, even physical illness as a result of the kind of seed they are sowing. Unlike Job, who suffered for the glory of God, they are being disciplined for sowing unrighteously, as was King David after he committed adultery and murder.

> If every Christian fully understood the law of sowing and reaping, his life-style would change dramatically. If I know that I will reap what I sow and more than I sow, I am more likely to sow love than hate, harmony than discord, compliments than criticism, generosity than stinginess and selfishness.[1]

God controls the return. It is He who returns a harvest of blessing. At His choosing He will also limit the return if He sees us selfishly profiting from the return rather than extending the work of His kingdom.

God's Word clearly indicates that misuse of His resources can result in a substantial shortfall in returns. Two passages from the Old Testament teach us about this through the experiences of the children of Israel.

In Micah, we find that when God's chosen people decided no longer to trust and obey Him, they soon learned that their sowing of crops was literally in vain. God chose to withhold His blessing because of their sin. God communicated His displeasure through His prophet:

> You will plant crops but not harvest them; you will press out the oil from the olives, and not get enough to anoint yourself! You will trample the grapes, but get no juice to make your wine (Micah 6:15, TLB).

Two hundred years later, following the captivity of the children of Israel in Babylon, God's people again neglected the Lord. They chose to focus on their selfish needs in Jerusalem, ignoring the fact that the temple lay in ruin. They were preoccupied with self-gratification and personal pleasure and filled with greed.

The first chapter of Haggai records the Lord's admonishment:

> Is it then the time for you to live in luxurious homes, when the Temple lies in ruins? Look at the result: You plant much but harvest little. You have scarcely enough to eat or drink, and not enough clothes to keep you warm. Your income disappears, as though you were putting it into pockets filled with holes!...You hope for much but get so little. And when you bring it home, I blow it away—it doesn't last at all.... I am holding back the rains from heaven and giving you such scant crops (Haggai 1:3-6,9a,10, TLB).

Many stewards are missing the special blessing of the Lord because they are not obeying the Lord's commands. Rather than distributing what God has given they hoard their harvest. They fail to remember Jesus' command:

> Don't store up treasures here on earth where they can erode away or may be stolen. Store them in heaven where they will never lose their value, and are safe from thieves. If your profits are in heaven your heart will be there too (Matthew 6:19-21, TLB).

This command is given for our good, not for our harm. The one who hoards treasure of any kind soon begins to take on the selfish view of the world. When this happens the steward's impact on his world is lost.

The farmer who sows seed must give up a treasure with the anticipation of multiplying what is given up. Sometimes we feel emotional pain when we are called to give up something. But Jesus makes us a fantastic promise:

> Truly I say to you, there is no one who has left house or brothers or sisters or mother or father or children or farms for My sake and for the gospel's sake, but that he shall receive a hundred times as much now in the present age, houses and brothers and sisters and mothers and children and farms, along with persecutions; and in the age to come, eternal life (Mark 10:29,30, NAS).

4. *Keep alert to growing conditions.* An alert farmer knows

the seasons. He is aware that the present environment has a great deal of influence on the harvest that is yet months away. He understands the effects of the temperature, the intensity of the sun, the wind, the rain—all of which have a significant impact on his crop.

By being sensitive to how environmental conditions can affect his crop, he is able to make compensatory decisions. You too need to be alert to the world's influence on that which you sow.

If you are extending love and concern to a hurting friend, watch for others who are not concerned for your friend and who may discourage rather than encourage him. You may have to go an extra mile to protect your investment of love and concern as it takes root in your friend's life.

5. *Focus on details.* An experienced farmer has an eye for detail. He is concerned about insects, weeds, water levels, crop diseases and chemical balance. Every day he examines the crop and decides when it needs water, fertilizer or insecticide. He is continually taking action to create and produce the maximum yield.

The farmer gives tender, loving care to what he has sown. He does whatever is necessary to guard against conditions that could thwart growth or eventually kill the harvest.

As you mature in your role as God's steward, you will be able to spot details that affect your harvest of righteousness. Using God's Word as your garden manual, learn to identify those conditions that can stunt the growth of what you sow—such as a negative attitude. Make corrections so you can realize a bountiful harvest.

6. *Reap the harvest.* The farmer's reward for sowing is reaping the harvest. An abundant harvest should never be stored. Except for a small amount that is used to sustain the farmer and his family and to provide the seed for the next planting season, the harvest is put into circulation. As other people are affected, their joy is also made full.

In God's timing you will be privileged to gather in what you have sown, and you too will be rejoicing. You will realize a return more than you can ever use. You will then have the privilege of circulating the harvest into the hands of others; and perhaps without knowing it, you will have sown again.

Paul gives us greater insight into the process and benefits of sowing and reaping in his second letter to the Corinthians. We've examined the principle of giving hilariously, which is covered in 2 Corinthians 8.

Now let's look at chapter 9 of 2 Corinthians (TLB) and glean more priceless nuggets regarding the harvest:

Verse 1:   I realize that I really don't even need to mention this to you, about helping God's people.

WHAT ONE SOWS AND THEN REAPS IS A MEANS OF DIRECT MINISTRY. THE HARVEST IS GIVEN TO HELP OTHERS.

☆   ☆   ☆

Verse 2:   For I know how eager you are to do it, and I have boasted to the friends in Macedonia that you were ready to send an offering a year ago. In fact, it was this enthusiasm of yours that stirred up many of them to begin helping.

AN ABUNDANT HARVEST PRODUCES EAGERNESS TO SOW AGAIN.
AN ABUNDANT HARVEST CREATES ENTHUSIASM AND HOPE IN THE HEARTS OF OTHERS.
AN ABUNDANT HARVEST STIMULATES OTHERS TO SOW AND WATCH FOR THEIR HARVEST.
AN ABUNDANT HARVEST PROVIDES THE ABILITY TO MEET NEEDS IMMEDIATELY.

☆   ☆   ☆

Verse 6:   But remember this—if you give little, you will get little. A farmer who plants just a few seeds will get only a small crop, but if he plants much, he will reap much.

AN ABUNDANT HARVEST IS DETERMINED BY HOW MUCH IS PLANTED.
AN ABUNDANT HARVEST IS BASED ON THE FARMER'S WILLINGNESS TO SOW FREELY.
THE ABUNDANT HARVEST CIRCULATED GUARANTEES A BOUNTIFUL RETURN.

☆   ☆   ☆

Verse 7:   Every one must make up his own mind as to how much he should give. Don't force anyone to give more than he really wants to, for cheerful givers are the ones God prizes.

THE DISBURSEMENT OF AN ABUNDANT HARVEST
RESTS IN THE HANDS OF THE STEWARD.
THE ABUNDANT HARVEST IS TO BE ADMINISTERED
BY HILARIOUS STEWARDS.
GOD IS PLEASED WHEN A HARVEST IS DISBURSED TO
MEET OTHERS' NEEDS.

☆　☆　☆

Verse 8:   God is able to make it up to you by giving you
everything you need and more, so that there will not only be
enough for your own needs, but plenty left over to give joyfully
to others.

THE CIRCULATED HARVEST HAS A HIGH YIELD TO
THE FARMER.
GOD GUARANTEES A BOUNTIFUL RETURN ON WHAT-
EVER IS GIVEN.
THE CIRCULATED HARVEST PRODUCES A JOYFUL
EXPERIENCE FOR THE GIVER.
THE ONE WHO SOWS, REAPS AND GIVES AGAIN HAS
MORE THAN ENOUGH TO MEET HIS OWN NEEDS.

☆　☆　☆

Verse 10: For God, who gives seed to the farmer to plant,
and later on, good crops to harvest and eat, will give you
more and more seed to plant and will make it grow so that
you can give away more and more fruit from your harvest.

GOD SUPPLIES THE SEED FOR THE FARMER IN THE
FIRST PLACE.
GOD PRODUCES THE HARVEST.
GOD WILL GIVE MORE SEED AND MAKE IT GROW.
GOD GIVES SO THAT THE FARMER CAN GIVE AWAY
MORE AND MORE OF HIS HARVEST.

☆　☆　☆

Verse 11: Yes, God will give you much so that you can give
away much, and when we take your gift to those who need
them they will break out into thanksgiving and praise to God
for your help.

GOD SUPPLIES ABUNDANTLY SO THAT YOU CAN
GIVE ABUNDANTLY.
GOD OFTEN PROVIDES AGENTS FOR HIS STEWARDS

WHO HELP ENSURE THAT ONE'S GIVING IS MEETING
GENUINE NEEDS.
THOSE WHO BENEFIT FROM OUR HARVEST SOW
THANKSGIVING AND PRAISE TO GOD.
AN ABUNDANT HARVEST PROPERLY CIRCULATED
REAPS AN ADDITIONAL HARVEST OF THANKSGIVING
AND PRAISE.

☆   ☆   ☆

Verse 12: So, two good things happen as a result of your
gifts— those in need are helped, and they overflow with
thanks to God.

A DISBURSED HARVEST ALWAYS RESULTS IN NEEDS
BEING MET.
A DISBURSED HARVEST ALWAYS RESULTS IN ABUN-
DANT THANKS TO GOD.

☆   ☆   ☆

Verse 13: Those you help will be glad not only because of
your generous gifts to themselves and to others, but they will
praise God for this proof that your deeds are as good as your
doctrine.

A DISBURSED HARVEST STIMULATES PRAISE TO GOD.
A DISBURSED HARVEST IS TESTIMONY THAT ONE'S
ACTIONS REFLECT ONE'S COMMITTED BELIEFS.
A DISBURSED HARVEST IS TESTIMONY OF GOD'S SAL-
VATION FOR MANKIND.

☆   ☆   ☆

Verse 14: And they will pray for you with deep fervor and
feeling because of the wonderful grace of God shown through
you.

A DISBURSED HARVEST WILL STIMULATE PRAYER
ON BEHALF OF THE DISBURSER.
A DISBURSED HARVEST DEMONSTRATES GOD'S
GRACE AT WORK THROUGH HIS PEOPLE.

☆   ☆   ☆

ECHO PRINCIPLE

As a young lad of six, I was introduced to what is known as
the echo principle. I remember the first time I experienced the
return of my voice.

My family had joined other members of our church for a picnic on the Colorado National Monument. At dusk, as the sun was setting into the west, Dad took me over to the edge of the cliff.

Enormous, dramatic sandstone monoliths reached from the valley floor to the darkening sky. Their shadows made them look even larger than their actual size.

Dad said, "Listen, Larry." Then he yelled toward the canyons and cliffs across the valley, "Hello, friend."

In seconds, the canyons called back, "Hello, friend; hello, friend; hello, friend." Never in my life had I heard canyons talk before, but these did!

Dad then yelled, "How are you?"

Again, the canyons responded, "How are you? How are you? How are you?"

Then Dad encouraged me to try it. I boldly yelled a six-year-old, "Hello," and listened excitedly.

"Hello, hello, hello," the canyons called back.

Whatever I said came back to me. Furthermore, what I sowed with my lips returned to me multiplied.

Everything we do—every word we say, every feeling we express, every dollar we give—will echo back to us multiplied. It is a law of the harvest. Therefore, how important it is to sow positive words, deeds and actions. Only as we sow seeds of righteousness can we expect God's blessings and a bountiful harvest.

It is important that we continue to give abundantly from what we have. Don't stop. There is never a time to quit sowing and reaping. To stop is to short-circuit the circulation process. As long as God provides you with seed to sow (and we will see later that you have over 75 varieties of things to sow), you should sow cheerfully, systematically and unto the Lord.

Ann Landers ran a poem in her column some time ago that seems to sum up the spirit we should maintain:

> "Go, give to the needy sweet charity's bread,
> For giving is living," the angel said.
> "Must I keep giving—again and again?"
> My peevish, petulant answer ran.

"Oh," said the angel, piercing me through,
"Just give till the Master stops giving to you."

Test your own farming ability now by working through your Key to Freedom, Exercise Nine.

Remember: *What you sow, you will reap!*

KEY TO FREEDOM

Exercise Nine

What do you want to plant? You have a wide variety of seed available to you—money, encouragement, wise advice, etc. Note here what you have decided to plant:

What do you expect to reap as a result of your planting? Describe what you believe the harvest will look like:

What are some things you might need to do to ensure an abundant harvest?

1.

2.

3.

4.

5.

Now begin. Plant your chosen seed. Pay attention to details as you begin to watch after your harvest. Review 2 Corinthians 9 and see what you can do to enhance your sowing and reaping process.

Chapter 10

My Father's Abundant Supply

While on a trip to the Northwest a few years ago, my wife and I needed to replenish our cash supply. Because we had an automatic bank withdrawal card, this was no problem to us. We simply found our bank's local branch, inserted our card in the automatic teller, pushed a few buttons, and instantly we had cash in hand to use as we needed.

Our daughter, Jessica, thought this was a great game. All Daddy had to do was push some buttons and, like magic, crisp new bills were delivered into his hands. During our trip we made several more stops at various branch banks in various cities. Each time I allowed Jessica to help me obtain the money.

Several months later as our family was driving across our home town, Pat and I were discussing the pros and cons of making a particular purchase that afternoon. "Larry," Pat said, "we would benefit from the purchase; but as I see it, we don't have the money now. I think we should wait."

Before I had a chance to respond, Jessica piped up, "Daddy, you can get all the money you need. Just go over to the bank and use that machine. All you have to do is press the right buttons."

From Jessica's view, there was an unlimited supply of money available to me. Although she knew very little about how banking works, she did understand one simple truth—the person who knew what buttons to push could receive ready cash.

PRINCIPLE 5

Jessica's response brings us to Principle #5:

My giving can begin to reflect the resources of my heavenly Father's household, not merely my limited resources.

Beside the fifth point of the star I have written: I can give from my Father's abundant supply.

My Father owns it all.

I can give from my Father's abundant supply.

My Father wants me to give hilariously.

My Father wants me to ask.

What I sow, I will reap.

As stewards, you and I have been given free access to God's unlimited resources. What He has is available to those who have the access code to His supply.

A few months ago, I learned a valuable lesson concerning my access code at my bank. This lesson also gave me some insight into accessing God's resources.

CARD NOT VALID

One Saturday afternoon I needed some cash. I went to the automatic teller machine, inserted my bank card in the appropriate slot, pushed the correct buttons and waited. Instead of money this time, I received a message: "Card not valid." I made a half dozen attempts, but each time the machine gave me the same short, not-so-sweet answer. Baffled, I went home that day without the money I needed.

On Monday I went to the bank to investigate my problem. The friendly bank teller checked my number. The account was authorized to accept my request. She examined the card. It appeared to be O.K. Now she too was confused, so we explained the dilemma to another employee of the bank.

"Do   you   work   at   the   Campus   Crusade   for   Christ administration center?" she asked me.

"Why, yes, I do," I replied.

"Then I'm sure I know the secret to your problem," she replied. "You have a security card key system that permits you to enter your building, rather than using a traditional key, don't you?"

"Yes," I replied.

"Do you carry your card key in your wallet?" she asked.

"Yes, it's right here." I took my billfold out and showed her my card key.

She explained that a magnetic field was built into the plastic card that identified me as one who was authorized to enter my office building when I placed the card in the appropriate slot.

My bank card was also magnetically coded to show that I was authorized to receive the bank's services. Under normal conditions, the bank card performed faithfully for me. However, when the magnetic field of my bank card came in contact with the magnetic field of my office card, the bank code was scrambled or erased.

Without my knowing it, my bank card had lost its authority to access my account. It looked and felt the same, but could no longer perform with the authority that it once had. Therefore, I had to obtain a new card.

As I walked out of the bank that day, I had a new insight into banking security—and into the importance of a steward living in the power of the Holy Spirit, with every known sin confessed.

CODE TO GOD'S RESOURCES

To tap into the resources of your heavenly Father effectively, it is necessary for you to choose to live your life in the power of the Holy Spirit. It is only the Spirit-filled steward who has unlimited access to God's abundant resources.

The vast majority of Christian stewards today live lives of defeat and frustration. Like my bank card, they are not capable of performing as they should. They may look as though they have it all together; but on the inside, they know that their access code has been scrambled. They are virtually worthless as far as Kingdom business is concerned.

A steward in this condition may still show up at all the right places. He can pray when called upon to do so. He may teach a Sunday school class. He may even give a little when asked to do so. He *appears* to be living a dynamic life.

It's only when he seeks to access God's unlimited resources that he painfully realizes he doesn't have the code number needed to withdraw from God's account. Something has short-circuited the system.

IS YOUR CODE NUMBER SCRAMBLED?

Are you living like a faithful steward on the outside while realizing that something is missing on the inside? Take heart. God does not delight in mediocrity. He is not satisfied with your living an average Christian life. He has unlimited power and provision available to you. God delights in seeing the supernatural expression of His power work in every facet of your life.

You can begin to live a dynamic life in the power of the Holy Spirit and to tap God's unlimited resources freely. I know this is true. I'm a walking example!

As a preacher's kid, I had a pretty good feel as to what a Christian should and should not do. I knew how to act the part, and almost no one knew I was only acting.

I knew that Jesus Christ was my Savior. I had put my trust in Him long before I started grade school. I also had a good grasp on Bible truth. During my first twelve years of life, I memorized hundreds of verses, thanks to my Mom. I could take on just about anyone in a memory quiz and win.

I was active in Sunday school and church throughout my teen years. I spoke in churches, led singing at youth rallies and recruited other teens to "get with it" spiritually.

But for the most part, my Christian life had no genuine joy or peace. I was living my life as an actor on a stage. Something was missing.

During my junior year at the University of Colorado, while majoring in theater, I finally came to the end of my emotional rope. I was tired of acting. I was tired of trying to make a good impression. I was tired of trying to live a Christian life that I knew was impossible to live.

Then I met two engineering students who were genuinely full of life. They gave me encouragement, love, time and friendship. I saw in their lives a dimension of the Christian life that I had never experienced. These guys were real!

One day I asked one of them why he seemed to be overflowing with love, joy, peace, interest in people, compassion and encouragement.

He explained to me that only weeks earlier he had learned how to allow God to control and empower his life. He shared with me that the key to the Christian life was not doing but being. He explained that every believer can be filled with and empowered by God's Holy Spirit by *faith*. The dynamic Christian life is not based on one's acting ability or on how one feels.

After that, I began to learn more about the Christian's source of power—the Holy Spirit of God Himself.

Being controlled and empowered by the Holy Spirit is the key to tapping the unlimited resources of God. As you submit to the leadership of the Holy Spirit, you become an Authorized Wealth Distributor. The one who is filled with and walks by faith in the power of the Holy Spirit is the one who can give freely without limitation, for he has the very life and power of God working through him.

I began to experience the reality of being set free to be all that God wanted me to be—not by acting or by the way I felt, but by trusting God to do what He said He would do if I only asked Him. By faith I asked Him to fill and control my life.

So that you can understand what was shared with me back in college, please take some time right now to turn to Appendix I. This message is so *critical* to the victory and joy you experience in your life, that I urge you to read it in its entirety before going on with this chapter.

SPIRITUAL BREATHING

As I began to apply these principles, my life took on an entirely new dimension. I was no longer limited to my own strength and my immediate earthly possessions. Now I was able to make withdrawals from God's riches and use the withdrawals to help others.

As I grew in my understanding of God's power, I learned that I need not look for mountaintop experiences to accelerate my Christian growth. All I needed to do was apply the principle of spiritual breathing. Applying this principle daily continues to give me an unlimited moment-by-moment supply of God's resources.

Spiritual breathing is simply exhaling the impure and inhaling the pure by faith so that one can continually experience God's love, power and forgiveness.

To *exhale* is to confess your sin. To confess means simply to agree with God concerning your sin. He is not surprised when you sin, for He was aware of your sin the moment it was committed. When confessing sin, or exhaling, name the sin, agree that it is sin, and thank Him for His forgiveness of that sin.

Claim His promise in 1 John 1:9 (TLB): "But if we confess our sins to him, he can be depended on to forgive us and to cleanse us from every wrong. [And it is perfectly proper for God to do this for us because Christ died to wash away our sins.]"

Genuine confession involves repentance, or a change in attitude or action—exhaling. By exhaling you get rid of those things that can limit the Holy Spirit's working in your life.

After you exhale, it is necessary to *inhale*—to surrender anew the control of your life to Christ and to receive the fullness of His Holy Spirit by faith. (Feelings are not a prerequisite to being filled with the Holy Spirit.) Just as you received Christ by faith, claim His power and resources also by faith.

Claim the command to be filled by the Holy Spirit in Ephesians 5:18 (TLB): "Don't drink too much wine, for many evils lie along that path; be filled instead with the Holy Spirit, and controlled by him."

Also claim the promise of God's Word in 1 John 5:14,15 (TLB): "And we are sure of this, that he will listen to us whenever we ask him for anything in line with his will. And if we really know he is listening when we talk to him and make our requests, then we can be sure that he will answer us."

You can breathe spiritually as many times as is necessary every day. This is your access code to keep God's power and resources flowing through your life to impact the needs of yourself and others. He will set you free to experience His power and *unlimited* resources.

UNLIMITED POWER

One of my hobbies as a teenager was a rather complex model train setup. I used to spend hours running my five engines and their cars around a 6' x 12' train table. On occasion, however, my entire train operation abruptly halted. Even though it had access to the Colorado Public Service Power Company, nothing worked.

When this occurred, I knew that somewhere on that intricate table layout, something was wrong. One time when it happened, I checked everything, but nothing seemed out of place. All the cars were on the tracks. From all appearances my trains should have worked.

After many hours of frustration, I decided to run a small magnet over every inch of the over 200 pieces of track. Eventually I found the problem—a tiny nail that was used to hold the track in place had worked its way out of its position and become lodged between the outer rail and the center track.

This little insignificant nail had caused a complete shutdown of my entire railroad for over two days. But once I removed the nail and turned on the transformer, the entire table came to life again. Power was once again flowing freely through the system.

In a similar way, sin in our lives can short-circuit our power supply from the Holy Spirit. The concept of spiritual breathing— exhaling and inhaling—can keep you free from obstructions and give you unlimited power to carry out your stewardship responsibilities.

POWER FOR A PURPOSE

Shortly before His crucifixion, Jesus told His disciples:

> In solemn truth I tell you, anyone believing in me shall do the same miracles I have done, and even greater ones, because I am going to be with the Father. You can ask him for *anything,* using my name, and I will do it, for this will bring praise to the Father because of what I, the Son, will do for you. Yes, ask *anything,* using my name, and I will do it! If

you love me, obey me; and I will ask the Father and he will give you another Comforter, and he will never leave you. He is the Holy Spirit, the Spirit who leads into all truth. The world at large cannot receive him, for it isn't looking for Him and doesn't recognize him. But you do, for he lives with you now and some day shall be in you. No, I will not abandon you or leave you as orphans in the storm—I will come to you (John 14:12-18, TLB).

Jesus then explained to them:

You didn't choose me! I chose you! I appointed you to go and produce lovely fruit always, so that no matter what you ask for from the Father, using my name, he will give it to you (John 15:16, TLB).

Think of it! You were chosen by God Himself as one of His stewards. You have been appointed to be productive in carrying out your tasks. You are given the authority to ask of the Father whatever you wish to carry out your tasks. *You are given the power to be all that God wants you to be.*

Jesus promised He would send the Comforter. The Comforter is the Holy Spirit—the Spirit of Jesus Christ Himself. Jesus was willing to die on the cross and then break the bonds of death because He was not satisfied merely to *walk with* His disciples. He wanted to *live through* His disciples! But because He could not take residence in sinful lives, He chose to pay the price of our sin. Once our sin was covered by His blood, He could move in.

AUTHORIZED WEALTH DISTRIBUTOR

Do you see now why you are an Authorized Wealth Distributor of God's unlimited riches? He has chosen to distribute all He is and has through His stewards. He seeks those who will allow Him to work His life freely through them. He does not force Himself on any steward; but when He has an available, Spirit-controlled steward, He freely gives Himself through that steward.

Think of it this way:

1. You are the only view of God's character that many people will ever see. How you act, what you say, and how you respond will either draw people to Him or cause people to turn from Him. As you are filled with the Holy Spirit, you reflect the very nature

of God to those you touch.

2. As a Spirit-filled steward, you are responsible to see that every resource He distributes through you gains maximum returns in bringing about His will.

3. The authority you have at present is part of your on-the-job training to prepare you to exercise additional authority with Him in eternity. He is training you to think as He thinks, love as He loves, give as He gives. How privileged you are to have a Teacher like the Holy Spirit. He wants you to succeed. You are His agent— His Authorized Wealth Distributor.

TWO APPROACHES TO GIVING

Your responsibility is to distribute God's resources to others. There are basically two ways to give:

Selective logical giving. This first form of giving is a counterfeit of the way God planned for His stewards to distribute His wealth and resources. Unfortunately, most stewards today are greatly limiting their access and distribution through this form of giving.

Selective, logical giving is based on the premise that there is a limited supply to be given. Therefore, it's important *not* to give—or at least give sparingly—for if you give freely, you very well might run out.

The Mazatec Indians of southwestern Mexico have an interesting approach to life, based on their concept of limited good. These people believe there is only so much good, so much knowledge, and so much love to go around. Therefore, if one gives himself to teaching another person how to do something, there is a good possibility that the teacher will drain himself of knowledge. To love a second child means you have to love the first child less.[1]

Many thousands of believers in our culture today seem to think the same way. Many act as if God is a limited resource.

Selective, logical giving has some basic characteristics:

1. This type of giving is based on what one can reasonably give. If giving something away will not greatly affect the inventory or disrupt a plan of action, then the giving *may* occur. If, on the other hand, it looks like giving will disrupt a plan of action, the

response is usually, "Sorry, I just can't help."

2. This type of giving may cause the giver to feel abused by people making requests because he feels over-extended. Have you ever felt you were being taken advantage of? If so, you likely were giving from a selective, logical viewpoint.

3. This type of giving meets needs, but the joy of giving is largely lost. Rather than experiencing excitement in helping meet a need, the selective, logical giver often feels empty or depressed after giving.

4. This type of giving is often viewed as a pledge or debt that must be paid. A friend once confided in me, "I made a pledge a few years ago. I have since changed my mind on the worthiness of the organization, but I'm a man of my word. Next month will be my last payment. I'm sure glad to be free of this burden." Selective, logical giving fails to rely on God's insight in making commitments.

5. This type of giving can be defined best as giving without seeking God's direction. This is the only way the unbeliever can give, for he is not in communication with God. At best he can rely on his and other people's knowledge and judgment, but he has no ability to tap God's wisdom and understanding.

Supernatural, Spirit-directed giving. The believer who is filled with the Holy Spirit has the privilege of giving in the second way—a supernatural, Spirit-directed way. To be able to give in this way is one of the greatest blessings one can experience from God. All it takes is an act of faith.

The steward who chooses to exercise his authority in giving is relying on God's specific direction to give. You're authorized to meet the needs that God lays before you.

This form of Spirit-directed giving is based on several truths:

1. God knows what is needed. He is aware of every need—spiritual, physical, mental, social, etc.

> So my counsel is: Don't worry about THINGS—food, drink, and clothes. For you already have life and a body—and they are far more important than what to eat and wear. Look at the birds! They don't worry about what to eat—they don't need to sow or reap or store up food—for your heavenly Father

feeds them. And you are far more valuable to him than they are. Will all your worries add a single moment to your life?

And why worry about your clothes? Look at the field lilies! They don't worry about theirs. Yet King Solomon in all his glory was not clothed as beautifully as they. And if God cares so wonderfully for flowers that are here today and gone tomorrow, won't he more surely care for you, O men of little faith?

So don't worry at all about having enough food and clothing. Why be like the heathen? For they take pride in all these things and are deeply concerned about them. But your heavenly Father already knows perfectly well that you need them, and he will give them to you if you give him first place in your life and live as he wants you to (Matthew 6:25-33, TLB).

2. God will enable each steward to give what He leads that person to give.

God is able to make it up to you by giving you everything you need and more, so that there will not only be enough for your own needs, but plenty left over to give joyfully to others. It is as the Scriptures say: "The godly man gives generously to the poor. His good deeds will be an honor to him forever." For God, who gives seed to the farmer to plant, and later on, good crops to harvest and eat, will give you more and more seed to plant and will make it grow so that you can give away more and more fruit from your harvest.

Yes, God will give you much so that you can give away much, and when we take your gifts to those who need them they will break out into thanksgiving and praise to God for your help (2 Corinthians 9:8-11, TLB).

3. Giving from God's resources does not limit the steward to the amount of his earthly resources.

Now I want to tell you what God in his grace has done for the churches in Macedonia.

Though they have been going through much trouble and hard times, they have mixed their wonderful joy with their deep poverty, and the result has been an overflow of giving to others. They gave not only what they could afford, but far more; and I can testify that they did it because they wanted to, and not because of nagging on my part. They begged us

> to take the money so they could share in the joy of helping the Christians in Jerusalem ...
>
> You know how full of love and kindness our Lord Jesus was: though he was so very rich, yet to help you he became so very poor, so that by being poor he could make you rich (2 Corinthians 8:1-4, 9, TLB).

When you give from God's resources, at His direction, you become the first to benefit. You grow in faith and obedience to the Lord. You experience firsthand His unlimited resources flowing through you to others.

Giving supernaturally does not rule out the use of logic. When you give supernaturally, you do not put your mind on a shelf. God created you with a sound mind. He has given you the capacity to reason and to think. He wants you to choose willfully to seek His counsel, obey His direction and rely on Him to supply others' needs through you.

God is waiting to bless you supernaturally. Yet He cannot bless disobedient stewards. I pray that you will choose to apply this truth in your life and to discover the dynamic life that God has prepared for you.

THE BOTTOM LINE

Supernatural, Spirit-directed giving boils down to your choosing to live by faith. Faith is the combination that unlocks your Father's fortune. Only as you exercise faith will your faith increase. The only limit to your tapping all that God has for you to give away is your unwillingness to trust Him, obey Him and act by faith.

Start by claiming God's promises. If you have never asked God to cleanse you and fill you with the Holy Spirit, you must start here.

Remember to breathe spiritually. This allows you to walk in the Spirit with freedom beyond all human comprehension.

Then by faith rely on the Holy Spirit to work in and through you. As an act of faith, thank Him for filling and controlling you and for giving through you—whether you feel it or not! Put your faith in God and His Word, and you soon will be experiencing the abundant life that only a faithful and trusting steward can experience.

Remember: *You can give from your Father's abundant supply*!

KEY TO FREEDOM
Exercise Ten

Turn back to Appendix I and review the simple outline concerning being filled with the Holy Spirit.

Do you understand this important truth of being filled with and controlled by the Holy Spirit? Your understanding of this truth is the secret to victorious living.

If this information is new to you, please commit yourself to reviewing these principles. Allow this truth to become a part of your heart and life.

Spiritual breathing enables you to live a Spirit-filled life every day. Learn to breathe spiritually the moment you see sin has entered your life.

If you know right now that you are filled with and controlled by the Holy Spirit, write a one-paragraph testimony of His power working in your life. Then sign and date the statement and keep it.

Chapter 11

Where the Rubber Meets the Road

Biblical principles are great to know, but what good are they if you can't apply them to your life in practical ways? Too many stewards are sitting before excellent Bible teachers, soaking up the Word of God, but souring because they are doing nothing with what they are learning except hoarding it for themselves.

The real test of stewardship comes when you are called upon to take action. If you are not breathing spiritually and walking in the Spirit, you could easily miss the opportunity to demonstrate effective stewardship.

In this chapter I want to help you get on track with practical applications of the five principles of God's wealth distribution system. Just reading about the principles will not make you what you want to be. I pray that this chapter will begin to help you live the life of a wise and thoughtful steward. Applying the content of this chapter will equip you to act.

There are seven steps you can take to begin applying what you have learned:

1. *Give yourself and your possessions to God.* Have you, as an act of your will, turned your life over to Him? Have you said, "Lord, I relinquish all rights to my life. Take me and put me to work as a steward for Your kingdom"? God is able to work only through the person who has turned the controls over to Him.

Have you given your possessions to Him? Yes, I know, He

already owns everything; but as an act of your will, have *you* turned everything over to Him? How about your health? Your job? Your family? Your hobbies? Your material accumulations? Your home? Your dreams? Your future? God can do a lot with a little if He has all there is of it.

2. *Recognize that God is your total and final supply of all you need.* The humanistic philosophy wants you to believe that you are the controller of your life. The world yells to you, "Work harder and you will obtain success. Your job is your source of provision. Your leisure time is your source of rest and relaxation."

It is because of God's continuous gifts to us that we live, breathe and have our being. Your income cannot make you happy. Your family and friends cannot provide you with genuine joy. God, and only God, is your total and final supply of all you need.

3. *Count on Him by faith to empower you with the Holy Spirit.* There is no one more miserable than a believer trying and striving to live the life of a steward in his own strength. God gave us the Holy Spirit so that we could be all that He planned for us to be. He planned for you to live a victorious Christian life. He planned for you to be His authorized wealth distributor. He planned for you to have His power plugged into your system.

My home in California was built over sixty years ago. Each room has no more than two electrical outlets, and until a year ago, we had a 15-amp electrical system. But then Pat and I decided to remodel our kitchen. An important improvement was an electrical upgrade to 110 amps. With this power upgrade, we now can use modern conveniences that previously were not available to us.

Wouldn't it be ridiculous for Pat and me to continue living as if the power were not there? We have an abundance of power. The Southern California Edison Company is ready to supply our needs. All we have to do is plug into the power source. Likewise, the power to live the victorious life as a steward of God is at your disposal. All you need to do is plug into the power which the Holy Spirit supplies.

4. *Begin to give according to His directions.* He has already provided you with hundreds of things you can give. Now it's a matter of your distributing what you have. God cannot provide you with more until you give away what you already have. As

you give what you have, you make room for more. God is then able to make a compensating deposit into your stewardship inventory.

Look for opportunities to give. If you are still wondering what you can give, the next chapter will whet your appetite and stimulate your mind to consider creative ways to give. There is no limit. To reap a harvest, however, you must consciously sow and watch for the return.

5. *Thank and praise God for the privilege you have of distributing His wealth and resources.* Nothing pleases our heavenly Father more than hearing expressions of thanksgiving and praise from His stewards. I am convinced that thanksgiving and praise unlock the gates of His storehouse more than anything else.

Thanksgiving demonstrates our humility and gratitude for all He does for us. Thanksgiving is an act of worship that demonstrates we are walking by faith. Even when, from our vantage point, the situation may seem bleak, we are told: In everything we are to give thanks; for this is God's will for you in Christ Jesus (1 Thessalonians 5:18, NAS).

Thanksgiving frees us from our earthly focus and helps us keep our minds and hearts on the things of God.

Praise is the language of heaven. Since we are a part of His kingdom, it is only reasonable that we communicate in the official language. Why? First, our heavenly Father is worthy of praise. Look at all He has done for us. He is the omnipotent Creator and Giver of everything. The psalmist put it to music with these words:

> Praise the Lord! Yes, really praise Him! I will praise Him as long as I live, yes, even with my dying breath (Psalm 146:1,2, TLB).

Second, we are to praise God for the many benefits and privileges He lavishes upon us. If you're having trouble remembering His benefits, take a look at Psalm 136 and Psalms 145 through 150. There is no way we could ever begin to acknowledge all the privileges and benefits He has extended to us, His children.

God also takes action when we praise Him. In 2 Chronicles 20:12, King Jehoshaphat found himself up against incredible circumstances. The armies of Ammon, Moab and Mount Sier had declared war on Judah. King Jehoshaphat called the people of Judah together and prayed:

> O our God, won't you stop them? We have no way to protect ourselves against this mighty army. We don't know what to do, but we are looking to you (TLB).

The Lord answered the request of His people. He instructed them not to be afraid. He promised deliverance without fighting. God had an incredible rescue operation planned for His people.

King Jehoshaphat decided there should be a choir prepared for battle. They were dressed in sanctified garments and instructed to sing a song of praise, "His Loving Kindness is Forever." The king appointed the choir to lead the people in praise and thanksgiving.

What happened? Praise unleashed God's power and provision for His people:

> And at the moment they began to sing and to praise, the Lord caused the armies of Ammon, Moab and Mount Seir to begin fighting among themselves, and they destroyed each other! (2 Chronicles 20:22, TLB).

If you are facing a problem, don't fret—praise God. The greater your challenge and the more difficult your circumstances, the more important it is to praise God and to express your thanks to Him for His provision for you. Every time you praise God, you are demonstrating faith in His ability to supply.

6. *Expect results.* You demonstrate faith when you watch with expectancy for the harvest of what you sow. As you give, be assured that God will return to you what you have given at the point of your need. You will also receive a multiplied return.

Remember, Jesus promises:

> For if you give, you will get! Your gift will return to you in full and overflowing measure, pressed down, shaken together to make room for more, and running over. Whatever measure you use to give—large or small—will be used to measure what is given back to you (Luke 6:38, TLB).

God controls the return. He determines when your giving is to return to you. He may choose to be very creative in how your return is delivered.

A few years ago, I had a major project due. It was a rather complex report that involved interviews, analysis and considerable creative planning and writing. But other responsibilities had kept me from giving it the attention it needed.

I was many hours from finishing the project, but the deadline had crept up on me—it was due within a day. The only way I saw to finish the task was to cancel everything else, accept no phone calls, ask my secretary to prepare for a long night of overtime, and get to work. So I asked that no one interrupt me; I was determined to get the project done.

When I was no more than fifteen minutes into the project, my intercom buzzed. At first I thought I'd ignore it, but I reluctantly picked up the phone.

"Larry, there is a call that I really believe you would want to take," my secretary told me. She assured me it would take only a few minutes.

Before I answered the call, I paused and prayed, "Lord, I'll give time to this matter now, but I'm counting on You to multiply back to me the time I give to help a brother in need."

I picked up the phone. "Hi, how can I help you?"

About an hour later, we finished our phone visit with prayer. As I hung up, I wondered how I was going to make up the time when in only a few hours the project had to be finished. I started to panic!

I called my secretary on the intercom. "Please, no more calls, not even from Pat! I've got to get going, or you and I will be here all night."

As I hung up, I said to God, "O.K., Lord, let's see You pull this one together. Thank you that You know more about this project than I do."

I expected to see God give me a quick course in Spirit-powered writing. But ten minutes into the task again, I saw that my thoughts were not jelling. Amidst my desperation, the intercom buzzed again. "Oh, no, not again. I said no more calls!"

"What's the problem?" I responded as I picked up the phone.

"It's Rick, and he's calling concerning the project you're

working on. I told him you asked not to be interrupted, but he said it was important to talk to you personally," my secretary told me.

I sighed and took the call. "Hi, what's going on?" I asked Rick.

"Larry, I've been doing some evaluation on the project and the deadline we are under. I'm not ready, and I know you've still got a lot to do; so I'm moving the deadline up by at least two weeks. Relax. I'll get back with you tomorrow so we can reschedule things."

That was over six years ago. There never was a follow-up meeting. The project was never completed. God didn't just extend my few hours that afternoon; He gave me multiplied time that I never thought I would see.

7. *Give again and again and again.* Don't play games with giving. Although there will always be a multiplied harvest, you should never give to get. Rather, give to receive to give to receive to give...

Think of giving and receiving as a continuous cycle. Never stop. What God gives to you is just what someone else needs. You have an unlimited inventory to draw upon. Use it freely. Your continuous giving will change your life as well as meet thousands of needs.

Be creative in your giving. Guard against hoarding. Have fun distributing what God has given to you.

As you take these seven steps, you are joining a special association of believers whom I have been referring to as Authorized Wealth Distributors. This is a network of Spirit-filled believers who choose, as an act of their will, to give freely to the needs of others.

As I have spoken to various audiences on stewardship, I have challenged them to make this commitment:

AUTHORIZED WEALTH DISTRIBUTOR COMMITMENT

By faith, I have given myself and my possessions to God and recognize Him as my total and final provider of all that I need. I hereby count on Him, by faith, to empower and control me with His Holy Spirit. I declare that I shall give according to His direction, expecting obvious results that will strengthen my walk of faith.

—————————————————————   ——————————————————

Signed   Date

Are *you* willing right now to take this step of faith and declare yourself an Authorized Wealth Distributor?

Authorized Wealth Distributors have been active in every culture since the first generation of man. As you study God's Word, you will find hundreds of examples of men and women who chose to trust, obey and give what they had to meet the needs of others. Some were famous. Most were average people like you and me.

AN AVERAGE WOMAN

Take the woman in 2 Kings 4:1-7, for example. She was a single parent with two young boys. Her husband died while attending seminary. He apparently left his wife with some outstanding debts. Because she was not able to pay the creditors, she was in jeopardy of losing her sons to slavery as compensation for the debt.

In desperation she turned to God's prophet, Elisha. She explained her dilemma and asked him what to do. Elisha responded by asking her what food she had in her house—a rather strange question considering her circumstances.

She explained that all she had left was one jar of olive oil. Not very much—but God took what she had and multiplied it. Elisha told her to gather all the pots and jars she could borrow from everyone in her neighborhood, take them into her home and close the door. She obeyed.

Elisha told her then to pour the one jar of her olive oil into another jar and set the filled jar aside. She was to continue filling the other containers until they were all filled.

As she gave from the one jar she had, God took care of the multiplication. One container after another was filled. The more she gave, the more she had. Only when the last jar was filled did the oil from the original container stop flowing.

From the abundant return of God's unlimited inventory, she

was able to sell the oil, pay her debt and free her boys from the threat of slavery. As an act of her will, through faith and obedience she became an Authorized Wealth Distributor for the Lord.

The issue is not what you have or how much you have; the issue is, What are you going to do with what God has given to you?

I'd like to share a few tips that will help you to be productive:

KEEP YOUR PRIORITIES IN ORDER

1. *Give to God. Keep your eyes on Jesus.* He's the best example you have. The more you focus on Him, the more effective you will be.

Keep walking in the Spirit. Yes, you will stumble. You will fall. But you can exhale and inhale and keep your heart and mind free from the distractions of the world. The Holy Spirit can work only through a clean vessel.

Keep saturating your mind with God's Word. The Bible is full of examples of giving and contains thousands of promises. The effective Authorized Wealth Distributor knows his procedures manual.

Keep asking God for direction. Ask Him what you should ask for. Ask Him for wisdom and insight in how to respond to needs. There will be times when He will tell you that someone else will meet the need. Be sensitive in asking and in listening.

Keep living a life of integrity. As a child of God, and as His steward, you should reflect the mindset of the Kingdom at all times—even when no one is watching you!

Keep walking in reverence and obedience to the Lord. Your desire should be to please the One who has called you to be a faithful steward. God is a holy God. Give Him reverence and obedience. Your life will be full of peace and joy as you respect His authority.

2. *Give to your family.* Nothing is sadder to me than seeing a steward stuck on the sidelines of life's greatest adventure because he hasn't given attention to his family.

Your family needs you to give to them. But please don't fall into the trap of giving them only money and material possessions. These are a poor substitute for giving *yourself.*

Focus special attention on giving your family many of the items listed in the next chapter. Be creative in giving yourself to them. Don't allow Satan the joy of messing up your model of effective stewardship to the world.

A special note to the husband. There is no way you can hire your responsibility to your family out to someone else. God has placed you as the senior vice president of your home and family. You cannot be an effective Authorized Wealth Distributor to a world in need if your wife and children are starving for what you have to give to them.

Remember, those closest to you spell love: *T-I-M-E*. Kids want a father, not simply a financial officer who shows up periodically to hand out the allowances. And your wife would much rather have a companion than an exhausted business success.

It's not just the amount of hours spent that makes the difference, but also the quality of the time spent. Ask God to give you balance in this area of life. Then give the balance away by the example you set in your home.

3. *Give to yourself.* Don't misinterpret what I'm saying. I'm not saying you should look out for number one or see how much you can hoard. By now you know this way of thinking is contrary to God's design of effective stewardship.

Any sensitive steward, however, must make sure he has personal time for getting his own batteries recharged. In order to give from your inventory, you need to have God's perspective. You need to be renewed. You need times to be alone so that God can talk to you. Be still. He wants to give you direction. By giving to yourself, you will be enriched and refreshed to give more effectively to others.

Be creative in this giving. Read at least one book each month that can help you in your work, your worship and your walk with God. Take walks in a quiet park or on a mountain trail. Soak in God's presence. Read a psalm a day or other passages that lift your spirit. Take a nap in a hammock or lie in the sun for an hour with your eyes closed.

What you do is not the issue. The key is taking time to be alone to think, to pray and to listen. Giving to yourself will multiply your impact in the lives of others. As a steward you need rest and relaxation on a regular basis.

4. *Give to the body of believers.* You won't have trouble finding people to give to. In fact, your challenge will be focusing on areas of greatest need. Determine where is the best place for you to focus your attention.

Just as a farmer focuses his seed sowing on a specific plot of land, you too will be more productive if you focus your giving. God touches each of our hearts in a different way. Sometimes our motivation is stimulated by a spiritual gift. If you know your spiritual gift(s), you will want to do things that maximize your gift(s).

Although there are many ways I can give, I often choose to focus my giving to gain the maximum impact possible. As you look at the body of believers that you know, don't forget the poor. Sometimes a gift of money is helpful. However, often you have other items in your inventory that can be equally helpful to them.

Don't get caught in the old trap of buying your way out of genuinely getting involved in the lives of believers. Remember, someday you may find yourself in a down-and-out state of affairs.

As a believer you have a responsibility to give toward helping to advance the cause of Jesus Christ through your church. You have much to offer. Find ways to stimulate growth in your church through your systematic, regular giving to that church body.

God will no doubt lead you to give to other Christian causes as well. Again, evaluate how you can accomplish the most through a focused approach. Select causes that reflect your heart. Then select organizations that you believe can multiply what you give.

Remember, giving doesn't mean just money. You may have much to offer by giving your talents, abilities, insight and experience. Giving a financial donation is only one of many ways you can give to most Christian causes. Remember these guidelines in your involvement in civic responsibilities also.

5. *Give to people whose lives you touch each day.* The vast majority of God's stewards don't live in a Christian environment. God has placed us in the dark and confused world to be salt and light. We are to stimulate growth of God's kingdom, and this means rubbing shoulders with the one who is not a steward of God's kingdom.

The ways to give are unlimited. The interest we show, the listening ear, the freshly baked loaf of bread, the bouquet of home-grown flowers or the skill to unlock the car door when the keys are left in the ignition are all ways to share God's love with a person.

But to stop at just doing nice things is to short-circuit genuine stewardship responsibility. You have the answer to life eternal! You have tasted of heaven! You know the Savior! You have the privilege of giving living bread to a hungry world!

You should be trained in how to witness to people and then look for opportunities to share how you found Jesus Christ with those God brings to you. Nothing is more rewarding than to be an agent for the kingdom of God by helping another person come to know Jesus Christ as his Savior and Lord!

Do you feel hesitant in sharing your faith? If you do, seek out training—through your church or a parachurch organization—in how to communicate your faith lovingly and effectively with others. Knowing how will give you new freedom in this important area of giving.

CULTIVATE POSITIVE ATTITUDES TOWARD GIVING

The attitude you choose to have concerning giving will have a direct correlation with your effectiveness in giving. Surrounded by so much greed and desire for materialistic benefits, you will want to cultivate a positive attitude. The attitude you have determines your success as a steward. To have and maintain a positive attitude about giving, I encourage you to follow the six guidelines listed below.

1. *Cast all your cares on the Lord.* If you find yourself preoccupied with worry, fear, loneliness or other things that drain you of your strength and positive view on life, give those cares to the Lord in prayer. He wants to take your burdens.

When you get discouraged, you cannot concentrate on meeting the needs of others. Give up your concerns by giving them to the Lord in prayer and trusting Him for the answers.

Dr. Henrietta Mears—who discipled such godly leaders as Bill Bright and Billy Graham—once encouraged some of her students to prepare a gift for God. In the package they were to put all those things that caused frustration and concern. She instructed them to wrap up the package and symbolically give it to Him. Then she said, "Once you've given it to Him, stop stealing His property!"

Let God have all those cares that limit your having a positive attitude. Cultivate casting your cares upon Him and live freely in His Spirit.

2. *Rejoice in the Lord.* Paul instructed the church at Philippi, "Rejoice in the Lord always; again I will say rejoice!" (Philippians 4:4, NAS). It often takes an act of our will to say thanks, to give praise and to rejoice. Sometimes circumstances seem so bad that the last thing we want to do is to rejoice. Yet God's Word simply says, REJOICE!

The rejoicing steward is able to see opportunities for ministry. He sees need. He's in touch with God's view of things. He is able to discern how God would have him respond. He's free to be salt and light. Cultivate a spirit of rejoicing.

3. *Give with others' needs in mind.* Years ago I attended a conference at which the late Dr. Raymond Edmond, then president of Wheaton College, was the keynote speaker.

One night he leaned over the lecturn and said, "Students, I would never have made it through school without claiming Philippians 2:4." And then he read out of his King James Bible: "Look not every man on his own things, but every man also on the things of others."

He then continued, "I justified cheating on my exams by using this verse until I learned that this verse had nothing to do with cheating and everything to do with caring. We are to look to others, find their need and step in and meet that need."

A more accurate translation of this verse reads, "Do not MERELY look out for your own personal interests, but also for the interests of others" (Philippians 2:4, NAS).

Watch. Look. Listen. Respond. Don't let opportunities slip through your hands. Cultivate watching for opportunities to give, and then give.

4. *Give your best.* I once heard a story of a wheat farmer in the Midwest who always supplied his friends on adjoining farms

with all the seed they needed to plant each spring. Year after year he insisted that they come to him and get their seed. He would not accept payment. All he asked was that they plant the seed he provided. After several years his fellow farmers were at last able to get him to explain why he insisted on giving them seed every year to plant.

With reluctance he explained, "I give you my best seed every year because I know that what you plant will affect my harvest. You see, my farm is in between the rolling hills. Your farms are on those hills. When our grain begins to grow, pollination occurs. If you don't have the highest quality of grain planted, it will affect my quality of return, too. I give my best so I can harvest the best."

To give less than your best when you give is a reflection on your heavenly Father's inventory. Cultivate the habit of always giving the best you can give.

5. *Give systematically and regularly*. Developing a positive attitude is like forming a good habit. It takes practice to be good at a skill. To be a good steward takes a commitment of your will, and it takes practice. Giving only occasionally does not sharpen the skill.

What would your life be if you were not systematic in other areas of life? Try not eating regularly. Try not paying your bills regularly. Try showing up at your job only when you feel like it—an hour here, an hour there. Systematic living gives us purpose, and systematic giving gives us freedom.

Just as a musician must practice daily in order to be successful, so too your expertise in giving will develop only with daily practice.

6. *Give willingly*. Our old sin nature would want to hold back. We all have a tendency to let someone else do it. Although God may direct you not to do something because He has another method in mind, I believe this is the exception rather than the rule.

When God instructed Moses to build the first mobile worship center (the tabernacle), He told Moses to invite the people to give whatever they had. In Exodus 35, God provides us a record of what the people gave. The tabernacle was constructed because of the time, talent and treasure of God's stewards responding to meet a need.

When Moses extended the invitation to give, the people willingly responded. Scripture records this for us:

> So the people of Israel—every man and woman who wanted to assist in the work given to them by the Lord's command to Moses—brought their freewill offerings to him (Exodus 35:29, TLB).

The King James version uses the expression, "whose heart made them willing." There was no sales program, no begging, no pressure tactics; they gave freely.

CULTIVATE GIVING FROM A WILLING HEART

As you cultivate your attitude as an Authorized Wealth Distributor by distributing God's resources, you will realize benefits that far exceed the investment you made:

You will be doing what God planned for you to do.

You will be meeting the needs of people.

Your needs will be met.

People who receive from you will be praising God.

People will be drawn to pray for you.

People will be giving glory to God—hilariously!

It is a privilege for me to extend a cordial welcome to you as a member of the Authorized Wealth Distributor Association on behalf of its Founder, the King of kings and Lord of lords!

KEY TO FREEDOM
Exercise Eleven

Turn back to page 148 and reread the Authorized Wealth Distributor's commitment. I encourage you to read this at the beginning of each day, focusing your attention on how God may want you to give yourself away.

Chapter 12

75 Ways to Give

About the only place you can find a genuine old-fashioned general store these days is in rural America. The days of the cozy store with the old potbellied stove and cracker barrel are all but gone. For most of us, the closest we will get to the old general store is visiting a high- priced tourist attraction or watching a rerun of "Little House on the Prairie."

Today our life-styles are dependent on one-stop shopping at mammoth supermarkets. Within these giant stores you can purchase about everything your heart desires—food, clothing, sporting goods, medicines, cosmetics, jewelry, garden supplies, office supplies, linens, housewares—the list goes on and on.

Our heavenly Father also operates a giant supermarket. In His store you will find everything pertaining to life and godliness. His inventory is unlimited, and His shelves are always stocked.

What's more, every product is on special—all of it is free! Almost two thousand years ago, Jesus Christ personally paid the price for your life membership. Your membership entitles you to shop as often as needed, with one restriction: You are allowed to stock up only if you have given your current inventory away. Only stewards of His kingdom are privileged to shop at this supermarket.

This store involves a unique network chain. Each member is called upon to set up a general store distributorship. It is through this network of distributors that the needs of the world are to be met. The philosophy of marketing is very simple: God to people, people to people.

I know you have shopped at this store many times—there is not a man or woman alive who does not benefit daily from items stocked on the shelves of God's storehouse. If you are like most shoppers, however, you easily can get into a rut and forget about the vast extent of the inventory available. Many end up using only a fraction of what is available.

To help you become better acquainted with the inventory that is yours for the taking, I asked forty-one members of my Sunday school class to make a list of what is available to believers.

I have compiled their answers into the following 75 categories, but as you read through this list, I'm sure you'll be able to add many more items!

"75 WAYS TO GIVE" SHOPPING LIST

1. ADVICE. Have you taken time lately to share your recommendation or thoughts with a person who needs a Spirit-filled steward's point of view on a matter?

2. AFFECTION. Have you expressed a tender feeling through a touch or a kind word to a person who is down? When was the last time you hugged someone outside of your family?

3. ANTICIPATION. Have you expressed excitement about someone else's expectation so that he knows you are pulling for him?

4. APPRECIATION. When was the last time you told someone how grateful you are to know him? Have you ever written a letter to someone, listing the ways that person has ministered to you?

5. BALLOONS. When was the last time you delivered a bouquet of balloons to a person to help express affirmation?

6. BELONGING. Have you reached out to help a person by including him in your group or making him feel more comfortable in his walk with the Lord?

7. BENEFIT OF THE DOUBT. Have you demonstrated faith in someone by giving him the benefit of the doubt, by looking at the person in a positive way, rather than in a negative way?

8. BLOOD. Have you given the essence of life recently to help those in need?

9. BOOK. When was the last time you gave a book to a person to help him through a circumstance or because you knew the topic would interest him?

10. BOUNDARIES. What action have you taken lately to help another person gain a sense of focus by setting up parameters for him?

11. CANDY. Have you taken time to buy or make a special sweet for a friend that says, "This reminds me of you"?

12. CARD. When did you last mail someone a card or letter that simply expressed you were thinking of him?

13. CARING. When did you last go out of your way to remember someone by showing genuine concern—maybe by mowing his lawn or buying some groceries? Are you aware that the way children develop empathy is by seeing parents care for others?

14. COACHING. Have you been willing to stand on the sidelines at times, encouraging someone else to grow and giving that person the spotlight?

15. COMFORT. Have you invested some comfort lately in the life of a grieving person? You may not need to give counsel; just your *being* there could be what the person needs most.

16. CONFIDENCE. Have you stopped to build someone up so that he could have confidence and courage to face the challenges of his life? Do you help others believe in themselves?

17. COUNSEL. Have you given time to provide biblical input and perspective to a friend who is trying to work through a major decision?

18. DEDICATION. Have you followed through on your commitment to a friend or a group, even when it meant relinquishing other enjoyable activities in order to fulfill your responsibility? Do you stick around when the going gets tough?

19. ENCOURAGEMENT. Do you provide positive feedback and cheer people on?

20. EXPERIENCE. Are you willing to share your experience with others so that they can be encouraged in working through

a challenge they have never faced before?

21. EYE CONTACT. When you talk with people, do you give them your attention by looking them in the eye? Your eyes can tell the other person how you really feel.

22. FAITH. Do you regularly give your faith away in such a way that people will recognize you as a Christian who walks in the power of the Holy Spirit?

23. FLOWERS. Have you delivered a living plant or a freshly cut bouquet of flowers to encourage someone—even when there was no special occasion? Dad, have you given a dozen carnations to your young daughter lately?

24. FOOD. Do you share with others what God has provided for your physical nourishment? A loaf of freshly baked bread or a sampling of homegrown vegetables, accompanied by a thoughtful note, can be a ministry in someone's life.

25. FORGIVENESS. Have you let someone who has hurt or offended you know that you do not harbor resentment and that he is forgiven? Your Father in heaven has forgiven you; can you do any less for others?

26. FUN. What have you done to stimulate fun among those you know? Have you planned a good time of recreation for someone or a group of people lately?

27. GENTLENESS. Are you mild in your manners and in how you deal with circumstances and people? When in a heated or complex discussion, do you give a quiet response rather than a harsh retort?

28. GUIDANCE. Are you giving leadership and direction to others in such a way as to stimulate them to grow?

29. HELP. Are you watching for opportunities to step in and lend a hand? Are you willing to risk your life to provide help to another?

30. HOLY SPIRIT. Are you walking in the Spirit and influencing the lives of others because of what the Holy Spirit has done for you?

31. HOPE. Do you demonstrate favorable and confident expectations about the future? Does your attitude stimulate others to have hope as well?

32. HOSPITALITY. Do you often go out of your way to make someone else feel needed and wanted? Are you always willing to set an extra place at your table for someone who drops in unexpectantly?

33. HUMILITY. Do you give yourself willingly to tasks that are not to your liking? Do you advertise your accomplishments, or do you seek to praise and build up others?

34. HUMOR. Do you look to find the light side of circumstances, seeking to turn a frown into a smile? Do you allow cheerfulness to dominate your life?

35. INSPIRATION. Do you give yourself and your ideas to others in such a way that you stimulate them to more creative efforts?

36. INTEGRITY. Does your life overflow with consideration for others, and with high character and stability? Do you tell the truth despite the circumstances?

37. JESUS. Do you give the gift of eternal life to those who have no relationship with God by showing them how they can have Jesus living in their lives as their Savior and Lord?

38. JOY. Does your life overflow with inner contentment and peace, even in the midst of difficult circumstances?

39. JUSTICE. Do you act in fairness to all and watch to see that fairness is extended to all?

40. KINDNESS. Do you give preference to others and show concern for others by reaching out to meet a need? Do you go the extra mile in meeting the need?

41. KNOWLEDGE. Do you use what you have been taught by others to encourage others to grow? Do you use the sound mind that God gave you in determining the course of action to take?

42. LAUGHTER. Do you freely express your joy and gaity to others? Laughter is excellent medicine for the troubled heart!

43. LISTENING. Do you give your full attention to others so that you can sort out wisely what you hear and provide insight and encouragement? Listening indicates to someone that you are truly concerned for him.

44. LOVE. Do you regularly express your affection for others,

letting them know that God loves them and that you love them too? How many ways can you show love today?

45. LOYALTY. Can others count on you to stand by them? How do you demonstrate your loyalty to your spouse? Your boss? Your pastor? Your friends?

46. MERCY. Are you there when someone needs you? When someone does something that hurts you, do you show mercy, just as the Lord has shown mercy to you? Do you extend kind, compassionate treatment to those who have not earned it?

47. MONEY. How free are you with the money you have? Do you use what you have to help others?

48. OBEDIENCE. How do you respond when someone asks you to do something you like to do? How do you respond when you are asked to do something that you don't like to do? How do you respond to God's directions in your life?

49. OVERTIME. Do you willingly give your time, talent or treasure above and beyond what is normally expected without making a big issue of it?

50. PEACE. Have you given a spirit of calmness in the midst of chaos and confusion?

51. PHONE CALL. Do you use the phone to comfort, encourage, listen to and express your love to others?

52. PLEASURE. Do you reflect delight and happiness to those with whom you associate? What can you do to brighten someone's day tomorrow?

53. POSSESSIONS. Do your possessions own you? Are you free to give what you have to meet the needs of others?

54. PRAISE. Are you always ready to give a compliment for a job well done? Do you regularly compliment God for His grace to you?

55. PRAYER. Do you regularly intercede for others? When you say, "I'll be praying for you," do you?

56. RESPECT. Do you give honor and esteem to those with whom you work? Are you courteous at all times? Do you give preference to those older than you?

57. RESPONSIBILITY. Can you give a task to someone and

express your trust that he will complete the task satisfactorily? Giving responsibility helps a person grow. Do you delegate authority to others to help them mature?

58. SECURITY. Do you give a sense of security to those who are fearful and concerned about their spiritual or physical environment? Your attitude in circumstances can give peace in the midst of a storm. When necessary, do you make the effort to protect others from physical or spiritual harm?

59. SELF-CONTROL. Do you exercise self-discipline at times when you would like to demand your way? Do you guard your words so that what you say does not cause disharmony and hurt?

60. SHARING. Do you ask others to join you in an opportunity to see something special? Do you give preference to others' needs when you have a need yourself? Are you willing to cooperate with others to accomplish an objective?

61. SMILE. Do you wear a smile that says, "I think you're special"? If you meet a person who's lost his smile, give him one of yours!

62. SONG. When was the last time you gave a person a little song to send him happily on his way? Do you sing songs of thanksgiving to God? He loves to hear you sing—even if it's only a melody in your heart.

63. SPIRITUAL GIFTS. Are you using your spiritual gift(s) to edify others? Are you aware of what spiritual gift(s) you have?

64. STRENGTH. Do you give the strength God gives you to uphold another's physical, spiritual or mental need? Sometimes this means showing a person how to lift a burden from his heart and give it to Jesus. At other times it means lifting a physical burden. The attitude in which you give conveys where your strength is coming from.

65. TALENTS. Do you maximize your God-given abilities by using them to stimulate and encourage others to good works? A talent hidden under a bushel will not bring glory and praise to God. You must use it, or you likely will lose it.

66. TEARS. Are you willing to give your tears to show that you too feel for the hurting? Are you free to laugh with those who laugh and weep with those who weep?

67. THANKSGIVING. Do you freely give thanks to those who have helped you accomplish an objective or task? Do you demonstrate a thankful heart to God for everything that occurs in your life?

68. TIME. Do you give time when you feel pressed for time? Giving time is a creative act from which all other forms of giving flow.

69. TRANSPARENCY. Do you allow others to see the real you, or do you hide your feelings from others? Do others sense your sincerity in what you say?

70. TRUST. Do you demonstrate to others that you can be trusted? Do you keep the problems others confide in you confidential? When you make a promise, do you follow through on it?

71. UNITY. When you see division, do you look for ways to transform strife into unity? If necessary, do you defer to the judgment of others to maintain unity?

72. WILLINGNESS. Do you volunteer to take on responsibility or to do something for someone else, even when it means you may be inconvenienced?

73. WISDOM. Do you make decisions based on your walk with God, or do you act only in light of your circumstances? Can people recognize you as one who continually trusts God for His wisdom?

74. WITNESS. Are you giving first-hand witness of God's continuous working in your life? Are you ready to give testimony of your faith at any time?

75. WORK. Do you give your best effort in completing a task, even when you'd rather be doing something else? Do you take on tasks that mean you must give out extra mental, spiritual or physical energy?

OPENING NEW VISTAS

Has this list of 75 ways to give opened up new vistas of giving for you? I hope so. You have all you need to get started on a new adventure.

While going through the list, did you notice that often you have to mix things together to be totally effective? Effective giving is like baking a cake; it is the combination of ingredients that produces the desired results.

There are three basic approaches you can take in giving. Each approach is of equal value; but as you mix the approaches together, you have *dynamic* giving.

THREE APPROACHES TO GIVING

1. *You can give yourself through person-to-person contact.* Immediate reward comes from genuine person-to-person, face-to-face contact. You see what the benefit of your giving produces. This is the most effective way to give yourself away.

2. *You can give yourself through voice contact.* Although circumstances do not always permit you to have face-to-face communication, the telephone allows you to give even when you can't be with someone. Many of the ways to give can be distributed via the phone.

3. *You can give yourself through the written word.* Letters and notes often can give encouragement, love, commitment, affection, advice, etc., more effectively than any other approach. A person can read what you have written time and time again. God has chosen to use His written Word as His prime means of instruction to us. We are able to study God's Word because it's in a form to be kept and studied with no time limits.

BALANCE FOR BEST RESULTS

For best results in giving, try to maintain a balance between these three approaches. If all three are being used effectively, you will enhance the distribution of God's inventory to others.

Ask God to make you a blessing through the ways you give. Ask Him to show you how you best can carry out your job description. Allow Him to be original in your giving. You've got a lot to give!

As you give, don't forget that you will never run out of things to give. Even when you feel you are in need, you have Jesus waiting to give to you and to others.

> Let us therefore draw near with confidence to the throne of grace, that we may receive mercy and may find grace in time of need (Hebrews 4:16, NAS).

You will never outgive the storehouse that belongs to God. You name it, He's got it. As an Authorized Wealth Distributor for the Lord, you will always have what you need when you need it!

KEY TO FREEDOM
Exercise Twelve

As you look through the list of 75 ways to give, write down some specific ways that you may give (you are not limited to that list, however). Who are some people who may especially benefit from what you have to give? Ask God to give you specific opportunities to give to those people.

Chapter 13

The Authorized Wealth Distributor and Money

For many years I have taught seminars on God's perspective of stewardship. I often ask those in attendance to respond with the first word that comes to mind when I say certain words. After dozens of such experiments, I've learned that there are some standard responses.

When I say "bacon," most say "eggs."

When I say "fire," most say "hot."

When I say "autumn," most say "leaves."

When I say "pool," most say "swim."

When I say "thirsty," most say "water."

When I say "give," most say "MONEY."

It seems we have programmed ourselves to think that giving is synonymous with money. Church bulletins often announce the offering as "worship by giving." The United Fund drive uses a catchy phrase: "Give the United Way."

If someone says, "I need to ask some people to give to meet this need," don't we automatically assume that he means he will ask people to make financial donations?

While we have seen that we have *much* to give to others besides money, it is still an important part of our inventory. In fact, the way in which we use our money says much about our values and our outlook on life. If you really want to know what someone is like, watch how he uses his money. Does he hoard it?

Does he spend it on impulse? Does he use his money to buy items of lasting value? Does he freely give his money to meet the needs of others? Does he have a plan for his money, or is it "here today and gone tomorrow"? Spending and saving patterns speak loudly about our character and personality.

MONEY TALKS

Did you know that you can identify a body of believers' maturity by how much money is given to meet the needs of that church body? If a church is meeting its budget, you are likely looking at a church of growing believers. If, on the other hand, the church is under financial strain because of a lack of funds, the church is probably made up of baby Christians or of self-centered, carnal believers.

A key indicator of the Spirit-filled believer is the way in which he views and manages his money. The steward who walks consistently in the power of the Holy Spirit will use his money to advance the cause of Christ. He is free from the obsession of selfishly hoarding his money. He is wise in the use of what God has entrusted to him.

Sad to say, our society's materialistic orientation has created a get-all-you-can-while-you-can mindset among non-believers and believers alike.

Even though $65 billion was given away to charity in the United States in 1983—an increase of 8 percent over 1982—this represents only 2 percent of individuals' total 1983 national income.[1]

The desire for the good life is robbing many stewards of the unlimited blessings that God has prepared for His Authorized Wealth Distributors. Thousands of believers have chosen to accept the limited rewards that the world offers, rather than the abundance that God has to offer.

EARN—SAVE—GIVE

Over a century ago, the famous circuit-riding preacher John Wesley was asked for his advice on the use of money. His response sums up the wise steward's beliefs, "Earn all you can....Save all you can....Give all you can." As an Authorized Wealth Distributor, you can follow this simple outline of money management.

Earn all you can by using the inventory that God has already given to you. Be creative. Work hard. Be wise. Use the sound mind that God gave you to turn your time and talent into the maximum return possible.

Save all you can by wise management of what you earn. Put your earnings to work so that they also will produce a return. Remember, your job description calls for you to manage what God has given to you. This means you are to make careful and prudent investment decisions. You want your earnings to gain the maximum return possible. Saving as a wise steward is not hoarding as old Mr. Scrooge did. A wise savings program keeps you from foolishly wasting what you earn.

If you are going to save all you can, you must become knowledgeable as to where and how to save. A wise steward should also live his life based on balanced accounts. You can have balanced accounts only through a good budgeting process. This is the way your earnings and savings are maximized.

Give all you can from the harvest of your earnings and savings. Your motivation as an Authorized Wealth Distributor is not to collect and store as a miser. Your motivation is to distribute the maximum for the glory of the Lord.

As a young boy, I learned of R. G. LeTourneau, the founder of the Caterpillar Tractor Company and of LeTourneau College. He lived on 10 percent of his earnings and savings and gave 90 percent to the work of God's kingdom. He demonstrated faithfulness as an Authorized Wealth Distributor!

You should be concerned about how your giving will be used to further God's purposes here on earth. Whenever possible investigate where you plan to give before you give. There are numerous questions that you should ask. With what you learn you can better determine how God wants you to respond. Here are ten categories of questions that can help get you started in wise evaluation of financial needs:

1. *Who is asking for a contribution?* Do you know the person? What do you know about him? Is he trusting in God or in your donation? Is he a person of integrity?

2. *Why is the gift being requested?* Do you understand the

need? What caused the need? Was it a result of poor management or was it stimulated by a real step of faith?

3. *Who will benefit from the need being met?* Will your gift be used to cover bad debts, or will lives be directly touched as a result of your help? How much of your gift will be used for overhead expenses? How much of your gift will be used for direct ministry?

4. *What do other wise stewards think of the need?* What counsel can you receive in your investigation to confirm or question the validity of the need? Who else has endorsed the request?

5. *Will your gift go to a bona fide institution or organization that is recognized for its service to people?* What do you know about the institution/organization? How long has it been in existence? What is its track record of ministry success? Is the purpose of the organization/institution clearly defined? Is its purpose consistent with your biblical views and convictions? Has it made available an accounting of expenses and income for its previous year?

6. *To whom does the one seeking the gift (individual, organization, or institution) focus its ministry?* Do you have a genuine interest in this type of need? Would a contribution from you stimulate your faith and personal involvement?

7. *Is the appeal for help creating high pressure or emotional guilt?* Do you feel that the appeal is trying to put a burden on you; i.e., "It's going to be your fault if we don't meet this need"?

8. *What kind of reporting can you expect to receive?* Can you see the results of your gift? Will you receive written communication regarding progress in meeting the need? What will be the lasting benefits of your gift?

9. *In what ways other than giving money can you be involved?* Is there also a need for other items in your stewardship inventory? Is the one seeking your help eager for your involvement or is he interested only in your money?

10. *Will your gift stimulate more giving?* Is there a way you can talk to other supporters of the cause? Can you help raise additional funds as a volunteer?

You will not necessarily get an answer to every question, but you should ask questions of the one soliciting your help, and he should be willing to answer each question as best he can. Some of the proposed questions require you to be a good observer. Read literature about the movement and seek the insight of others.

As an Authorized Wealth Distributor, you should not give blindly with no sense of stewardship accountability. You should always give with the goal of seeking to advance the work of God's kingdom business here on earth. He has called you to reflect, reproduce, reign and manage with His authority. You are His agent. Use your authority wisely.

Giving money should stimulate a time of great hilarity. You should thoroughly enjoy transferring money from your inventory to the inventory of others. Hilarity does not negate the tremendous responsibility you have in wise disbursement of resources.

A few years ago, I interviewed a man of great wealth. He was a genuine Authorized Wealth Distributor. He received great pleasure from helping meet needs. As we visited together, he confided to me, "Larry, I have found that the more God blesses me financially, the more responsibility He gives to me to ensure that what is given is properly used. It is not easy to give God's resources away. I must trust God for more insight, wisdom and understanding than ever before. My giving must result in lives being reached for my Savior."

THERMOMETER OR THERMOSTAT?

The way in which you give your money is a reflection of your character. The way in which you manage your money tells the world more about you than your words can ever express. It tells, for example, whether you are a thermometer or a thermostat.

A thermometer provides only a report of the surrounding temperature. It has no ability to change the circumstances. It merely tells what's currently taking place. A thermostat, on the other hand, not only reports but also triggers action that *changes* circumstances. A thermostat regulates the environment.

The steward who is not actively distributing his money is missing out on the opportunity to help *change* his environment through changing people's lives. Christians today may give a lot of other things, but many of them hold on to their billfolds so tightly that they miss the joy of being totally free and effective

172 GIVING YOURSELF AWAY

for God. Don't allow the focus on money to rob you of total victory as a Christian.

MONEY IS A TEACHER

Giving money will teach you more about the principles we've learned in our study together than any other single thing you can give. Money is something tangible. You can see it, feel it and experience its power and influence. God has provided us with a medium of exchange so that we can give and receive more efficiently. Money is not evil; only the *love* of money is evil.

God uses money to teach us how to trust Him. As we see God works through our money management, we can understand how He also works through our management of other items in our stewardship inventory.

It is sometimes difficult to see how giving love, for example, returns in a multiplied harvest of more love. However, when you give something as tangible as money, you can easily calculate the return. Money is the Authorized Wealth Distributor's tutor. Through this item you learn the dynamics of walking by faith, trusting Him on the return and obeying His direction. God is ready to teach. Are you ready to learn?

God never promised to provide excessive material possessions to every steward. He promised to meet every steward's *needs*. The amount of money a person has does not determine his happiness and peace. What one does with what he has is the great determining factor in the test of stewardship.

Jesus says:

> Don't store up treasures here on earth where they can erode away or may be stolen. Store them in heaven where they will never lose their value, and are safe from thieves. If your profits are in heaven your heart will be there too (Matthew 6:19-21, TLB).

AMOUNT MAKES NO DIFFERENCE

Despite the dollar amount that we have in our personal portfolio, we are to be obedient in our use of what is there. Here is what God's Word admonishes:

Stop loving the evil world and all that it offers you, for when
you love these things, you show that you really do not love
God; for all these worldly things, these evil desires—the craze
for sex, the ambition to buy everything that appeals to you,
and the pride that comes from wealth and importance—these
are not from God. They are from this evil world itself (1 John
2:15,16, TLB).

Disobedience in this or any other area of stewardship may
result in the chastening of the Lord. I have known believers who
hoarded their money and lavished material possessions on their
family members. They soon lost interest in the Lord and then
began to reap conflicts with spouses, children, friends, and others
as they too turned from the things of God. Disobedience under
any circumstance is not worth the destructive results.

The children of Israel who returned from captivity in Babylon
to Jerusalem had a responsibility before the Lord to rebuild His
temple. But rather than being obedient stewards, they became
selfishly preoccupied with their own affairs. They reveled in their
prosperity and forgot their responsibilities. We find God's chastening in the first chapter of Haggai:

Is it then the right time for you to live in luxurious homes,
when the Temple lies in ruins? Look at the result: You plant
much but harvest little. You have scarcely enough to eat or
drink, and not enough clothes to keep you warm. Your income
disappears, as though you were putting it into pockets filled
with holes! (Haggai 1:3-6, TLB).

You hope for much but get so little. And when you bring it
home, I blow it away—it doesn't last at all. Why? Because
my Temple lies in ruins and you don't care. Your only concern
is your own fine homes. That is why I am holding back the
rains from heaven and giving you such scant crops. In fact,
I have called for a drought upon the land, yes, and in the
highlands, too; a drought to wither the grain and grapes and
olives and all your other crops, a drought to starve both you
and all your cattle, and ruin everything you have worked so
hard to get (Haggai 1:9-11, TLB).

The Lord chastens those who are disobedient in their
stewardship. But those who are obedient reap the abundance of
His provision. Guard yourself to use your money, possessions,

time and talent for His glory and according to His plan. You can count on God's blessing as you faithfully fulfill your job description as a wise and sensitive steward of God.

WHAT ABOUT TITHING?

Do you tithe? If you do, why do you tithe? How much are you to tithe? Do you like to tithe? Are there any benefits to tithing?

I find that the vast majority of Christians today know very little about the tithe or its purpose. Unfortunately, even many churches view tithing as simply a funding scheme to help the church meet its budget. Pastors seldom teach the biblical purpose of tithing. Getting people to tithe is viewed as an uphill battle that is rarely won.

Yet I have found that those individuals who do understand the concept of tithing are *excited* about giving in this way. They do not—as others often do—give grudgingly, out of a sense of obligation and pressure.

Let's see what tithing is all about.

ONE-TENTH?

The word "tithe" means one-tenth. Tithing is simply giving 10 percent of your income to God. But the real question is, Why do it?

Attorney David Jackson of Evergreen, Colorado, spoke at a Christian financial seminar in California in 1981. *The Los Angeles Times* covered the seminar and quoted him as follows:

> The good Lord has entrusted certain assets to you and made you an agent . . . . The Master has a duty to cooperate with you. He will indemnify you and compensate you. Real estate agents get 7% to 10%; attorneys, maybe 33% to 40%. God has said you can have 90% agency. With generosity like that, don't you feel bad about limiting it to 10%?[2]

Think about it. As an Authorized Wealth Distributor, you are an agent for the King of kings. All you have belongs to Him. You are to distribute through sound management all that He has entrusted to you. His request is that you give only 10 percent back to Him. You manage and distribute the other 90 percent.

What a deal! What a tremendous privilege and honor! God trusts you so much that He allows you the responsibility and privilege of managing 90 percent and returning only 10 percent to what I call Central Kingdom Administration. You are, of course, free to give much more, but your agency agreement calls for only 10 percent.

To have a better understanding of the tithe, let us see what God's Word has to say about this fantastic concept.

IT STARTED OVER 4,000 YEARS AGO

The first tithe recorded in Scripture was given over 4,000 years ago—over 425 years before God gave the Law to Moses. Abraham returned from a successful battle to the city of Salem, the current location of Jerusalem. There he was met by Melchizedek, the king of Salem, who brought nourishment to strengthen him after the battle.

According to Genesis 14, Melchizedek was also the priest of the Most High God. Melchizedek blessed Abraham by saying, "The blessing of the supreme God, Creator of heaven and earth, be upon you, Abram; and blessed be God, who has delivered your enemies over to you" (Genesis 14:20, TLB).

Abraham then gave Melchizedek a tenth of all he had won in the battle that day. Out of gratitude to God, he gave it freely and willingly. Melchizedek never asked for it. Abraham simply gave it. As I see it, Abraham really gave *God*—by way of Melchizedek—an agency fee of 10 percent as an expression of his gratitude for His divine leadership in the battle.

JACOB'S TITHE

The next example we have of tithing is found in Genesis 28. Jacob, as you may recall, eventually had to flee his home because he tricked Esau out of his birthright. Resting one night during his journey, he dreamed of a staircase that reached from earth to heaven. Angels of God went up and down the staircase.

In the dream, God appeared to Jacob and promised him the land he was sleeping upon, many thousands of descendants, and protection wherever he went. When he awoke the next morning, Jacob built an altar at this location and made this vow to God:

> If God will help and protect me . . . I will choose Jehovah as
> my God! . . . and I will give you back a tenth of everything
> you give me! (Genesis 28:20,22, TLB).

Jacob took the initiative to commit 10 percent of what he had
to God. God did not require it of him. Jacob willingly offered it.
He chose to put God first and demonstrated his commitment with
his tithe.

THE LAW REQUIRED TITHING

Years later God gave His Law to His people. By now God's
promise to Jacob in Genesis 28 had become reality. When God
gave His Law to the nation of Israel, He included the provision
of tithing:

> You must tithe all of your crops every year. Bring this tithe
> to eat before the Lord your God at the place he shall choose
> as his sanctuary; this applies to your tithes of grain, new
> wine, olive oil, and the first born of your flocks and herds.
> The purpose of tithing is to teach you always to put God first
> in your lives (Deuteronomy 14:22,23, TLB).

> A tenth of the produce of the land, whether grain or fruit, is
> the Lord's, and is holy. If anyone wants to buy back this fruit
> or grain, he must add a fifth to its value. And the Lord owns
> every tenth animal of your herds and flocks and other domes-
> tic animals, as they pass by for counting. The tenth given to
> the Lord shall not be selected on the basis of whether it is
> good or bad, and there shall be no substitutions; for if there
> is any change made, then both the original and the substitu-
> tion shall belong to the Lord, and may not be bought back!
> (Leviticus 27:30-33, TLB).

The tithe was required by God of the people. It was a means
of paying for the cost of operating their government—a theocracy.
God appointed the Levites to be in charge of all matters pertaining
to civil and religious government. With the tithes they collected,
the Levites managed the governmental affairs, maintained cities
of refuge, supervised religious worship and education and took
care of all widows and orphans.

But the tithe for the nation of Israel was not just 10 percent!
The people were required to give 10 percent two times each year

and a one-third tithe each year. The average required giving by the Law was now 23 percent per year!

In addition to the required tithes—their income tax, if you will— the people also gave free will offerings. On numerous occasions, people gave these special offerings, not because they had to, but because they wanted to.

THEY BLEW IT

About four hundred years before Christ was born to redeem us from sin, the nation of Israel forgot God's commands. Their lives were no honor or reflection of God's holiness. They had badly blown it! God spoke to His people through the prophet Malachi:

> "For I am the Lord—I do not change. That is why you are not already utterly destroyed [for my mercy endures forever]."

> "Though you have scorned my laws from earliest time, yet you may still return to me," says the Lord of Hosts. "Come and I will forgive you."

> "But you say, 'We have never even gone away!'"

> "Will a man rob God? Surely not! And yet you have robbed me."

> "'What do you mean? When did we ever rob you?'"

> "You have robbed me of the tithes and offerings due to me. And so the awesome curse of God is cursing you, for your whole nation has been robbing me. Bring all the tithes into the storehouse so that there will be food enough in my Temple; if you do, I will open up the windows of heaven for you and pour out a blessing so great you won't have room enough to take it in!"

> "Try it! Let me prove it to you! Your crops will be large, for I will guard them from insects and plagues. Your grapes won't shrivel away before they ripen," says the Lord of Hosts. "And all nations will call you blessed, for you will be a land sparkling with happiness. These are the promises of the Lord of Hosts" (Malachi 3:6-12, TLB).

God is saying: Put Me first; obey Me; I will bless you. This promise of God is as true today as the day He first gave it to His people. God does not change—before the Law, during the Law, or after the Law.

JESUS AND THE TITHE

At the appointed time, Jesus Christ came. Did He throw out the Law? No, He fulfilled all of the Law. He never once rejected what had been established. He provided a way for mankind to meet the requirements of the Law. Only through accepting Jesus Christ as Savior can one put God first.

Jesus gives us freedom to be all God planned for us to be. No longer are we in bondage to sin. God's Holy Spirit sets us free to respond to Him by faith. Giving a tithe then becomes a joyful testimony of our faith.

REAL PURPOSE

In Deuteronomy 14:23 (TLB), we learned the real purpose of the tithe—it hasn't changed and never will:

> The purpose of the tithing is to teach you always to put God first in your lives.

Tithing is your tutor. God is not going to starve to death if you don't give Him His rightful agency fee. He won't lose out, but you will.

If you don't give to Him at least 10 percent, I can guarantee that you will very soon forget you are an Authorized Wealth Distributor. You will forget you are free to live a victorious and abundant life.

Look at tithing this way: This is your regular refresher course that reminds you who you are and what you are to do. As you set aside God's agency fee on a regular basis, you are recognizing Him to be first in your life. When you recognize Him to be your number one priority in the area of money, all the other areas fall more easily into line.

Pat and I started tithing as a couple the first week we were married. In all our years of marriage, we have never gone hungry. We live very comfortably. We have never been caught up in hoarding, nor have we been preoccupied with materialism. We are free because we recognize God to be our first priority in life, starting with our income. Over the years we have been so blessed that we have chosen to increase our tithe considerably. The more we give to Him, the more we always seem to have.

PUTTING TITHING TO THE TEST

A young couple with two children lived in a small, northern Colorado town. They owned an appliance business, but business wasn't good.

Times were tough for the little community in the mid-1950s. Like many others the young couple had their backs against the wall. Their financial problems overwhelmed them. No matter what they tried, there wasn't enough money to meet even the family's basic needs.

Then, on a cold and wet October day, they met a Christian businessman who was in the area on a business trip. They shared their despair with him. After they told him how tough things were, he asked them one simple question, "Are you tithing to God from what you now make?"

"No," they responded, "there's no way we can give to a church when we are not sure we can even feed our kids!"

"Well," the businessman replied, "if you're not giving God what's rightfully His, it's no wonder you're about to starve."

Then he proceeded to explain tithing to them. He challenged them to give God His agency fee first out of whatever income— large or small—they received. "Try tithing for eight weeks and see if you don't see a difference in your financial position," he challenged the couple.

After the businessman left, the young couple decided to try this wild idea. After all, on what they were making, 10 percent wasn't going to make that much difference. They decided to take 10 percent off the store profits each day and set it aside in a jar.

After a few days, they had collected several dollars. They decided to attend the small church down the street and give their tithe there. They seldom attended any church, but it seemed reasonable that God's money should be taken to a place of worship. They had sent their kids there on occasion, so they decided they would go during their eight-week experiment with God.

At first, things seemed to go from bad to worse financially. Nevertheless, on the days they sold something in their small store, they set aside God's 10 percent agency fee.

Four weeks went by. From their perspective, they were losing 10 percent and not gaining a thing. Their Thanksgiving feast was beans and potatoes.

Then it was three weeks before Christmas. Surely, they thought, people would come to the store to buy gifts. December had always been a good sales month. This time, however, most people just looked and wished. Some days there wasn't a single customer.

The couple's frustration now turned to anger. "Why is this happening? It's not fair," they cried. The wife was ready to wring the businessman's neck!

The husband had similar feelings but responded, "We made an eight-week commitment. The eight weeks are over in two weeks—December 24. When it's over, that will be the end of this experiment; but we've got to stick to our word till then."

Christmas that year was hardly one to look forward to. The husband went to the nearby woods and cut a small tree. His wife made paper decorations with the kids—but there wasn't a single gift to go under the tree. For Christmas dinner, there would be more beans.

On the morning of December 24 they opened the store. Throughout the day, people stopped by to look, but not to buy. When it was time to close that night, only a couple of dollars of profit had been made. God got a quarter.

That night the couple bundled up the kids to go to church. They trudged through the blustery cold, snowy night to the Christmas Eve service—and to put in their last tithe.

At the close of the service, they greeted the church friends they had made over the course of the last eight weeks. Then they headed home. The kids ran ahead, full of excitement for what they would find under the tree on Christmas morning. The young parents walked home without speaking. They knew there would be nothing under the tree.

As the parents walked up to their home, just behind the store, the kids were waiting. Dad pushed the door open, and the kids rushed in.

"Mom, what is this?" they yelled. The kitchen table was covered with every kind of food you could imagine. The kids opened the refrigerator and, to their amazement, it too was full of food. On the center shelf was a big turkey with all the trimmings, just waiting to be put into the oven.

The kids dashed from the kitchen to their small living room. "Look at this," they screamed. The tree was beautifully decorated with lights and glass ornaments. Under the tree were more than a dozen wrapped gifts for everyone in the family.

The parents were overwhelmed and confused! Where did all of this come from? Never once did they tell anyone in their community of their need or of their tithing experiment.

The next morning, after the gifts were opened, the husband received a phone call. "Merry Christmas!" greeted the caller. "Do you still have that electric range in your store? My husband gave me the money to buy it. If you still have it, could you deliver it tomorrow morning?"

That was just the beginning. In the first three weeks of January, the young couple did more business in their store than they had done during the previous three months! And to this day, they have no idea where the food and gifts came from that Christmas Eve.

Yes, this is a true story. They knew the businessman didn't provide their Christmas that year. When they told him of their tithing experiment over a month after Christmas, he was not even aware that they had started tithing after his challenge. In fact, he had all but forgotten about their conversation that day in October.

Some will say that their tithe experiment and the events on Christmas Eve and the days following were just a coincidence. But I think not. I believe that God prepared a blessing for them because they chose to put Him first.

God did use an Authorized Wealth Distributor to fulfill this need— but the couple will have to wait until they are in heaven to learn the name of their benefactor.

Although they understood little of what was happening, God was true to His Word:

If you do, I will open up the windows of heaven for you and pour out a blessing so great you won't have room enough to take it in! (Malachi 3:10, TLB).

TRY IT

If you have never experienced God's return through tithing your income, why not initially try it faithfully for eight weeks? There is nothing magical in the length of time, but an eight-week period allows you to watch God do some amazing things.

As you do, let God be original in how He chooses to bless you. Don't play games with God with an I'll-do-this-if-You-do-that attitude. Put Him to the test and watch Him keep His promise.

As you take the tithing challenge, remember that you are not doing this to get ahead or to help God out of a financial crisis. *The purpose of tithing is to teach you always to put God first in your life!*

CREATIVE GIVING

Tithing is a place to start—not a place to stop. In addition to giving God His agency fee, there are other creative ways to give financially that can stretch your faith. I have listed four.

1. Faith promise giving. The concept of faith promise giving has become popular today because of the testimony of Oswald J. Smith, of the Peoples Church in Toronto, Canada. Today, tens of thousands of stewards throughout the world are experiencing the adventure of giving by faith.

Faith promise giving has its roots in 2 Corinthians 8:5. Paul wrote of how the Macedonia Christians, despite their hard times and limited financial resources, gave by faith to meet the needs of the church in Jerusalem. These stewards in Macedonia were the first to give witness to faith giving:

Now, brethren, we wish to make known to you the grace of God which has been given in the churches in Macedonia, that in a great ordeal of affliction their abundance of joy and their deep poverty overflowed in the wealth of their liberality. For I testify that according to their ability, and beyond their ability they gave of their own accord, begging us with much entreaty for the favor of participation in the support of the saints, and this, not as we had expected, but they first gave themselves to the Lord and to us by the will of God (2 Corinthians 8:1-5, NAS).

The Macedonia stewards wanted to be meaningfully involved in the needs of the Jerusalem church. They were already giving what they had. No doubt they were giving their agency fee. But they wanted to do more. They believed God for the ability to give beyond their human ability. Giving beyond your ability is what faith promise giving is all about.

Faith promise giving is counting on God to provide a specific amount that is beyond your current ability to give.

Faith promise giving is not cash resources. Cash is what you have now. Although your commitment must become cash to be given, faith promise giving does not rely on current available assets.

Faith promise giving is not a pledge. A pledge is a horizontal commitment between a person and an organization with the objective of meeting a need. A pledge is based on ability to pay out of known resources over a prescribed period of time.

Faith promise giving is:

1. based on a decision and a desire to participate in what God is doing;
2. an act of faith, for the decision you make is based on future resources that you do not currently have;
3. a promise to God that you will give from your inventory as He supplies you from His resources;
4. believing God to supply from His resources as you make a decision to participate in meeting a need.

In 1972 I learned of the concept of faith promise giving. Since then, Pat and I have participated every year in some faith promise challenge. God has been faithful to supply from His resources time and time again.

Since 1972 I also have been privileged to challenge well over 300,000 people with the principle of faith promise giving. Time and time again, God has rewarded those who trust Him by meeting their commitment.

In my experience I have found there are only three reasons

that an individual would not see a faith promise commitment realized:

1. Failure to pray the commitment in (they forgot about it).

2. Lack of sensitivity to God's provision (God provided it, but they chose to use it for something else).

3. A faith *guess* was made (rather than a step of faith, it was a leap into the unknown, with no frame of reference to God's provision in the past).

If you are challenged to make a faith promise commitment, I encourage you to respond only if you sense God has given you a genuine desire to be involved in the need presented. Don't respond out of pressure. If you have a desire to be involved, then ask God what steps He would have you take that would stretch your faith.

The amount He lays on your heart may shock you but will likely be a figure that you can believe God for. As you sense God's leading about an amount, make the commitment. Then ask God to make you sensitive to His provision. Pray regularly for the need you are committed to help meet, and watch God provide!

I shared the principle of faith promise giving at a banquet one evening in Orlando, Florida. During the dinner I met a young couple who had faced some difficult times in the housing construction business during the previous nine months. We had a good time of discussing how God always provides for His children.

That evening I challenged those in attendance to join in the adventure of faith promise giving. I thanked them for coming and dismissed the two hundred guests. The young couple came up and asked to talk further with me.

"We feel we should respond to your challenge to make a faith promise commitment, but this is new to us," the young husband said. "Could you explain the principle to us again?"

I replied, "If God has given you a desire to be financially involved, then I encourage you to take a step of faith. I recommend that your commitment be a stretch of your faith but also a figure that you can visualize God meeting as you trust Him," I told them. In my mind I was thinking that $25 to $50 a month would be a good place for them to start.

"O.K.," the husband said. Then his face lit up. "We really have a desire to see God use us. We want to go for it." He sat down at the banquet table, took out his response card, filled it in, put it in the envelope I had provided them, sealed it and gave it to me. "I'm trusting God to work through us," the husband told me. "As He does, this is His. Thanks so much for helping us, Larry."

We shook hands, said good-bye to one another, and they headed out the door to their car.

An hour later my associate and I were working through the many responses. As I opened the envelope from the young couple, I discovered that they had committed $1,000 a month for the following twelve months! I was stunned. All I could think of was the difficult times they had experienced. How were they going to see this faith promise realized? Oh me of little faith!

About two weeks later, I arrived back at my office. Amidst a pile of mail awaiting my attention was a letter from my new friends at the banquet:

> Dear Larry,
>
> We want to thank you for introducing us to faith promise giving. We are already beginning to see God work.
>
> Last night my partner and I were closing out last month's books. We were able to take a profit for the first time in eight months. My wife and I then sat down and paid all of our bills. When everything was paid, we discovered we had $1,000 left over. God impressed us to send this immediately—His first provision of our one-year commitment to Him.

Enclosed in the letter was a check for $1,000. Since then they have not only met their commitment every month, but have also written of numerous other giving opportunities God has provided for them.

Faith promise giving is not limited to a specially selected group of Authorized Wealth Distributors. Any believer, regardless of age or financial position, can join in this adventure that results in needs being met and dynamic spiritual growth for the participant.

When you give in this manner, you begin to experience the

true dynamics of principle five on the five-pointed star, "I can give from my Father's resources."

2. *The Lord's account.* Have you ever considered opening a special account at the bank, separate from your personal operational account, where you deposit all funds that are available for God's kingdom business? Stewards who have done so report that it is one of the most exciting things they have ever done.

One couple I know is close to setting aside a triple tithe each month. From this they pay their first tithe to their local church fellowship. Their second tithe is designated to missions organizations for projects and missionaries. The third tithe is kept in the account without designation so that they are free to give as a special need is brought to their attention—whether it be an emergency request from a missionary, or a sack of groceries for a needy person in their community.

Whatever is deposited in this special bank account is used only for direct ministry for the Lord. Whenever they receive extra funds, they always triple tithe to this account before making other decisions with the remaining money.

Having a Lord's account is a tangible way to recognize your stewardship over God's financial resources. It becomes a constant reminder that God entrusts His resources to His stewards. Is God leading you to establish a special Lord's account?

3. *Planned giving.* What plans have you made to manage your affairs after you have been called home to heaven? Every Authorized Wealth Distributor should have a plan for the future. If you don't plan for the future, you are not fulfilling your responsibility as a faithful steward.

Although most of your giving should be done while you are living, no doubt God will take you home to heaven before you do everything you would like to do. To ensure that stewardship responsibilities are handled properly, it is necessary for each adult steward to have a Last Will and Testament prepared. This document will become the last words you have to say! What you choose to say and the directives you wish to give are therefore very important.

Through your will you should give testimony of your faith in Jesus Christ. You should also declare your authority as an

Authorized Wealth Distributor and give specific instruction as to who should be granted the authority to take the material and financial inventory that you are leaving behind and to continue to manage it for God's kingdom business. Next to your birth certificate and marriage license, your will is the most important document you will ever have. Don't leave for heaven without it!

If you die without a will, you forfeit all rights to distribute the inventory and responsibilities you leave behind. Only through a will can you speak with authority here on earth after you have entered heaven.

You will need help in preparing a will. Seek out a Christian attorney who understands biblical stewardship. With his assistance make the decisions that would be an honor to your heavenly Father. The attorney will provide legal expertise that will help you wisely make your last authorized wealth disbursement here on earth.

4. *Other ways to give possessions.* You are not limited to giving only cash. You can give other possessions that can be sold by qualified recipients. Anything you hold in your inventory can be given. To maximize such giving, you need the assistance of people skilled in the areas of handling such gifts.

For example, you can give art objects, automobiles, stocks and bonds, life insurance, stamp collections, land, jewelry and precious gems, etc.

Seek out professional counsel to determine how best to give items of this nature. If you hold legal ownership on something, there is a way for you to give it away.

Giving your money and your related possessions is where the rubber meets the road. Paul's instruction to young Timothy should be the standard of the wise and sensitive steward:

> Tell those who are rich not to be proud and not to trust in their money, which will soon be gone, but their pride and trust should be in the living God who always richly gives us all we need for our enjoyment. Tell them to use their money to do good. They should be rich in good works and should give happily to those in need, always being ready to share with others whatever God has given them (1 Timothy 6:17,18, TLB).

KEY TO FREEDOM
Exercise Thirteen

If you have never tithed in the past, why not start setting aside at least 10 percent of your gross income, beginning with your next paycheck or allocated income? TEST this truth for eight weeks and see what happens.

In your own words, describe why it is important to tithe (according to Deuteronomy 14:23):

After eight weeks have passed, list the results of your tithing experiment. What has this taught you about God?

Chapter **14**

Take Six Steps Forward

A re you ready for graduation? There comes a time in each of our lives when we've got to graduate from one stage of experience to another. The time has come for you to begin to use the new knowledge and understanding you have gleaned about giving.

Do you feel that you are ready to face the world as a Spirit-filled Authorized Wealth Distributor? There is no comprehensive exam to take. There is no cap and gown to be rented or worn. All you need to do now is walk boldly into your world and distribute what God has given to you.

Commencement is not the end. Commencement is the beginning of a new quality of life! As you move ahead, go as a steward who can be recognized as trustworthy in the task God has for him.

God has filled your life with an inventory of His riches. You need nothing else. Each item that He's given to you is a tool to be used to glorify His name. The moment you choose not to recognize items of your inventory as tools, they become idols. Maximize what you have. Use it, or lose it!

NEW PERSPECTIVE

Do you now have a new perspective on God-given desires? Do you now have a different view of the world of greed and need around you? Are you now more sensitive to how easy it is to get trapped in the fog of circumstances? Do you now know what to do to get free of that fog?

Where is your new focus? Do you now have a new sense of direction so that you no longer run from clump to clump like my old pony, oblivious of the goal? Are you delighting yourself in the Lord and allowing Him to meet your needs, wants and desires? Are you now comfortable in your submissive role to your heavenly Father?

And that job description—do you feel you have a better understanding of what is expected of you as a steward of the King of kings? Do you now have a handle on how to reflect, reproduce, reign and manage for your heavenly Father?

Do you have an understanding of God's principles of wealth distribution? Let us recall the five points of the star:

I trust that you have taken time to complete each Key to Freedom exercise. Reading a book does little for you unless you personalize its content in some way. The exercises at the end of each chapter are provided to help you internalize the content you have read.

WHAT NOW?

If you don't begin to use what you've learned, you will soon lose confidence in your ability and will cease to be on the cutting edge of faith that gives you the dynamic flair so needed in our troubled, confused world.

Here are eight ways to develop your skills as an Authorized Wealth Distributor:

1. *Practice.* You can never become really good at something unless you practice, practice. This means you need to develop

habits of regular, systematic giving. You need to have a plan.

My greatest concern is that you will treat your stewardship responsibilities as something you turn on or off like an electric light. With no system, no plan, no procedure or no goals, we can easily end up living haphazard lives.

If we were haphazard in living, we would either starve to death or go bankrupt within a month. What would life be like if you decided to get up every day whenever you felt like it? If you chose to go to work only when you were in the mood? If the kids went to school only when they wanted, and stayed home the rest of the time? Without systems, plans, goals and procedures, life would be a continuous debate.

Make plans to give. Decide what to give and follow through as a regular practice. The more often you give, the more effective you will be in giving.

As you practice giving, think quality! Don't give table scraps. Remember: What you sow, you will reap.

GIVE YOUR BEST

I once heard a story about a rich man who desired to be a genuine giver. One day he decided to ask a poor builder to build him a beautiful home overlooking the valley below. It was a lovely setting—a grand location for a mansion.

He explained to the builder what he wanted. He gave him plans and specifications. He told the builder he wanted the very best materials that money could buy and the highest quality workmanship he could deliver.

"I want this to be a really fine home. Spare no cost in building the very best," he explained.

The man then told the builder that he was going on an extended trip and would not return until after the elegant home was completed. The builder reasoned with himself, "What an opportunity to get rich! With him gone, I can cut corners and come out ahead!"

The builder proceeded to build; but rather than using the best materials, he cheated in every way possible. He used inferior products and did shoddy work. He was able to pocket a considerable sum as he did far less than his best.

After some time had passed, the rich man returned. The builder delivered to him the keys to the new home. He explained what a beautiful home he had built and referred to the quality of his workmanship to deceive the rich man.

"I'm so glad to hear this report," the rich man said, "I am indeed glad it was built with such care and thoughtfulness, because I have intended all along to give it to you when it was finished. The house is yours! Here, you take the keys. Move your family into your new, well- built home!"

As a steward don't cheat yourself. What you give will return to you. Practice, practice, practice!

There are numerous ways to do this. Tell others what you have learned. Share your testimony of how your life has taken on a new perspective since you've learned about way-of-life stewardship. Give your friends a copy of this book as a special gift.

2. *Become proficient in using the skills God has given you.* What do you really enjoy doing? God's Word teaches that each person who accepts Jesus as his Savior is given one or more spiritual gifts. You may wish to read the two major passages in the Bible regarding these gifts: Romans 12:4-8 and 1 Corinthians 12.

God gives each of us special abilities specifically to help others and to build up the church. You may be blessed with the ability to teach. Someone else may have a special ability to lead or perform services of help or mercy. Learn about your spiritual gift(s) and then develop them to your full potential.

You are responsible to use your spiritual gift(s) to meet the needs of the body of Christ. No, this doesn't mean you can forget the other gifts. It does mean, however, that you can specialize.

Some stewards have the gift of evangelism for example; others do not. This, however, does not mean that the one who has the gift of evangelism need not be concerned with teaching or showing mercy. Likewise, the steward who does not have the spiritual gift of evangelism is still commanded to share his faith and should look for opportunities to do so. But as each of us develops a degree of specialization in doing one or more skills, we can then use that ability to multiply God's kingdom business here on earth.

3. *Learn all you can about managing your finances.* Every steward should work diligently to become mature in matters related to finances. There is much to learn. Without education in this area, you may feel inadequate and ill-prepared to help others. Without proper insight and training, you will be unable to manage your financial affairs for maximum results. Inefficiency in money management is a reflection on your ability to manage other items in your inventory.

Proper money management will allow you to do more with what has been entrusted to you. You will be recognized as trustworthy by your heavenly Father if He sees good stewardship in this critical area. In the appendix at the end of this book I have listed several resources to help you in the area of financial management.

4. *Learn how to maximize your time.* The best way to find tips on maximizing your time and talents is through reading. Become an active learner. Focus on books that help you grow in your stewardship responsibilities. I personally try to read a minimum of one educationally oriented book each month.

God has given us a treasure through books. We are blessed abundantly with books by Christian authors on every subject imaginable.

Begin a reading list. When you hear of a good book, jot down the title and the author's name. Begin reading regularly. Use your church library. Read, read, read!

To get you started in this reading adventure, I recommend you get two books. These will help you maximize your stewardship skills:

Managing Yourself by Steve Douglass

Making the Most of Your Mind by Steve Douglass and Lee Roddy

Both books are published by Here's Life Publishers and are available now at your local Christian bookstore.

5. *Become an aggressive Authorized Wealth Distributor in your church and community.* There are numerous ways to do this. Tell others what you have learned. Share your testimony of how your life has taken on a new perspective since you've learned

about way-of-life stewardship. Give your friends a copy of this book as a special gift.

Will you allow God to use you to stimulate more stewardship awareness in your church? You may not be a born leader, but that doesn't mean you don't have influence on those who give visible leadership.

What is keeping you from volunteering to teach a four- to six-week course for a small group or in a Sunday school class based on the content of this book?

Why not invest some time, your hand at writing, and a few stamps and write for resource material from the addresses listed in the appendix? Why not begin building a library of quality material which deals with stewardship of one's time, talents and treasures? Check to see what your church library currently has. If you don't find a section on this subject, make it your project to create one, working in cooperation with your church librarian.

There are excellent cassette tapes available on this subject. All the organizations listed in the appendix have tape series. When you write, inquire as to how you can obtain their seminars on cassette tapes.

6. *Husbands and wives, work together as an Authorized Wealth Distributor team.* Nothing is more rewarding than to be involved as a couple in a worthwhile endeavor. This does not mean you do everything hand in hand, but it does mean you have common interests and continue to encourage one another. To be effective as a couple, let me suggest three ways to get started.

First, take a planning weekend together. If you have children, get a babysitter for two nights and three days (an entire weekend). Select a quiet resort-type area where you can be alone to think, talk, pray and relax together. The location should have nice restaurants nearby. Wives are not to cook on planning weekends!

Before you go, determine together what your agenda will be. What will you discuss—the discipline of the kids, frustrations in your communication, your schedule of activities for the next six months, ways to put into practice your responsibilities as Authorized Wealth Distributors, or other things? The list should not include more than three or four items.

Take appropriate materials that will be helpful in your

planning. If, for example, you were going to focus some time on your stewardship as a couple, you may want to take your copy of *Giving Yourself Away* so that you could discuss the various exercises together.

Another book I recommend is the newly published *Secrets of a Growing Marriage*, written by Roger and Donna Vann (Here's Life Publishers, available at your Christian bookstore). It is a high quality, family album type of book that will guide you in planning just such a weekend and will provide you with a personal permanent record of your getaway.

The purpose of a planning weekend is to enhance communication between husband and wife. Sometimes the process of communication is difficult, but it is always well worth it. Give yourselves to each other. Be transparent with each other. During one weekend, in how many of the 75 ways listed can you give to your spouse?

Why not put one planning weekend into your schedule every three or four months (or at least every six months)? This get-away time could be the most valuable investment you ever make in each other's lives. And if you feel your marriage needs some special help, don't hesitate to seek professional Christian counsel. Get things back on the track!

Second, attend a family conference. I recommend that you attend a Family Ministry Conference as a couple. These are excellent conferences that are held throughout the United States.

Family Ministries was established as a special ministry of Campus Crusade for Christ International some years ago because of the recognized need for help in marriage communications. Pat and I have benefited from our attendance at one of these seminars. You will, too.

Family Ministries also offers an excellent tape series on various topics that deal with family relationships. For more information write:

Family Ministry
200 South University, Suite 100
Little Rock, AR 72205
Phone: 501-661-0366

Third, begin a Bible study together as a couple. Begin to study something together as a couple that will enrich your lives spiritually. I'm not talking about heavy Bible study where the husband teaches the wife. I suggest something simple that gives you a springboard to other discussions.

For example, you may want to discuss a different psalm together each day. Or, you may want to use a study guide, such as *PROMISES, A Daily Guide to Supernatural Living*, by Bill Bright (published by Here's Life Publishers, San Bernardino, California). This book gives one promise from God's Word for each day of the year. It also includes some insights to reflect upon and a suggested action point based on the promise for the day.

HOW YOU LIVE IS UP TO YOU

Isn't it great to know that God is original with each of us? I'm thankful that each steward is one of a kind. I cannot tell you how to live your life. The life-style you choose is totally between you and your heavenly Father.

However, keep one thing in mind. You are to live your life for the glory of God. You are to seek first His kingdom. Recognize that everything you've been blessed with is still His. He is counting on you to use all His gifts for the furtherance of His plan on earth.

Edmund Burke once said, "All that is needed for evil to triumph is that good men do nothing." I believe you now know what to do. It's now just a matter of trusting God and obeying His Word. Continue to evaluate ways you can give to meet the needs of others. Continue to seek to bring men and women into a relationship with Jesus Christ. Always seek ways to multiply your influence through giving your time, talents and treasures.

You are now a vital part of a growing network of believers who believe they can make a difference for the Lord. If we as members of this network each choose to do our part, we can be assured of victory. United as a network of Authorized Wealth Distributors, we can see the world reached with God's love and forgiveness. In the process we will be demonstrating that our trust in God is reality. Remember, our actions speak as loud as our words.

As a steward you are created to find your maximum fulfillment in living a life that is free from the cares of this world. As
you maximize your inventory by giving yourself away, you are
free to give glory to God. You can experience heaven on earth as
you trust and obey Him.

WE CAN HELP CHANGE THE WORLD

We as Authorized Wealth Distributors have what it takes to
help change our world for the good. Our network has all that is
needed. In our inventory is the technology, the materials, the
strategies, the manpower, the expertise,the money—everything—
that is needed to meet the physical and spiritual needs of 4.7
billion people living on our small planet. Now it's only a matter
of giving what we have away and thereby glorifying God.

The bottom line is attitude. God wants to use you to reflect
His power and glory. Are you available?

In the midst of the barren desert between Los Angeles and
Las Vegas, stands a 300-foot tower. On the top of this tower rests
a black receiver that is 45 feet high and 23 feet across, surrounded
by 70 heat-conducting tubes.

The tens of thousands of people who drive across the desert
during daylight hours see a brilliant ball of fire glowing from the
top of the tower. This is the world's largest solar-powered electrical
generating station—Solar One.

How can a black receiver turn into a glowing ball with a
temperature exceeding 1,175 degrees F? The tower has no ability
to generate power by itself. The secret is on the ground.

On the desert floor surrounding the tower are 1,818 computer-
controlled frames. Each frame holds 12 giant mirrors that track
the sun each day from the time it rises in the East until it sets
in the West. The sunlight strikes these mirrors, known as heliostats.

The mirrors in turn reflect the sunlight onto the black receiver
at the top of the tower. The heat generated at the receiver is
transformed into electrical energy through a system of thermal
storage and a turbine generator. Power thus is generated from
the sun.

This process is possible only because a network of mirrors reflects sunlight onto a helpless receiver. When the network is working in harmony, power is generated.

REFLECTING THE SON

In many ways you and I as Authorized Wealth Distributors are like the heliostats on the desert floor. Our responsibility is to receive gifts from our heavenly Father. Our task is then to transfer what we have received to others. When we are available to receive, and we then give what we have received, we are obedient stewards.

We are reflectors of the Son. As we transfer what God freely gives to us on to meet the needs of others, we fulfill His plan for our lives. When we each choose to give, we are linked together in a dynamic network that has the potential of changing the world. Just think of what power can be unleashed for God's glory when the giving energy of a worldwide network of Spirit-controlled Authorized Wealth Distributors focuses on the needs of our sinful world!

But such a network is going to be effective only when each of us personally chooses to become a giver, rather than a taker. Leave the completion of the networking up to God. Your priority concern should be to carry out your job description as a faithful steward. Are you allowing God to work His will through you? Are you willing to give yourself away through the maximum utilization of your time, your talent, your treasure? If so, you are about to experience the freedom of an eagle as he soars in the heavens.

APPENDIX I

Have You Made the Wonderful Discovery of the Spirit-Filled Life?

WHY ARE SO FEW CHRISTIANS FILLED WITH THE HOLY SPIRIT?

Basically, the problem involves the will. Man is a free moral agent. He was created by God with a mind and will of his own.

God would be breaking His own spiritual laws if He *forced* man to do His bidding. At the time of conversion the will of man is temporarily yielded to the will of God. In Romans 10:9, Paul tells us that, if we confess with our mouths Jesus as Lord, and believe in our hearts that God has raised Him from the dead, we shall be saved. Man must be willing to "repent", which means to turn from his own way to go God's way, before he can become a child of God. However, after conversion, the heart frequently loses its "first love". The radiance and glow that accompanied the spiritual birth experience are gone, and many Christians no longer walk in "the light as He Himself is in the light" (John 1:7). They no longer seek to do the will of God, but for various reasons have chosen to go their own way. They have chosen to work out their own plan and purpose for life. Believing themselves to be free, they become servants of sin and finally they say with the apostle Paul in Romans 7:19,20,24:"For the good that I wish, I do not do; but I practice the very evil that I do not wish. But if I am doing the very thing I do not wish, I am no longer the one doing it, but sin which dwells in me. Wretched man that I am! Who will set me free from the body of this death?" There is no one more miserable than a Christian out of fellowship with Christ.

In this spiritual condition there is no longer any joy in the

Christian walk, no longer any desire to witness for Christ, no concern for those who are desperately in need of the forgiveness and love of our Savior.

What are the reasons, then, that one who has experienced the love and forgiveness that only Christ can give, one who has experienced the joy of His presence, would reject the will of God and choose to go his own way? Why would a Christian sacrifice the power and dynamic of the Spirit-filled life in order to have his own way?

There are several reasons:

A. *Lack of knowledge of the Word of God:* God's Word contains glorious truths concerning the relationship that the Christian has with the Lord Jesus Christ, God the Father and the Holy Spirit. Every Christian is a Child of God (John 1:12). His sins have been forgiven and he may continue to be cleansed from all sin (1 John 1:7) as he continues in fellowship with Christ. God the Father, Son and Holy Spirit actually dwell in the heart of every Christian, waiting to empower and bring each child of God to his full maturity in Christ.

B. *Pride*: Pride was the sin of Satan (Isaiah 14:12-14), and the first sin of man as Adam and Eve wanted to be something they were not. "God is opposed to the proud, but gives grace to the humble" (1 Peter 5:5).

C. *Fear*: "The fear of man brings a snare" (Proverbs 29:25). One of the greatest tragedies of our day is the general practice among Christians of conforming to the conduct and standards of a non-Christian society. Many are afraid to be different; ashamed to witness for the one "who loved us and gave Himself for us."

D. *Secret sin*: We may be able to hide unconfessed sins from our friends and others, but we cannot hide them from God. "Would not God find this out? For He knows the secrets of the heart" (Psalm 44:21). However, if we confess these sins to God as the Lord directs us, we are forgiven and cleansed (1 John 1:9).

E. *Worldly-mindedness*: A love for material things and a desire to conform to the ways of a secular society keep many Christians from being filled with the Holy Spirit. Every Christian should make careful and frequent evaluation of how he invests his time, talents and treasure in order to accomplish the most for the cause of Christ.

F. *Lack of trust in God*: Many Christians have a fear that amounts almost to superstition that, if they surrender themselves fully to God, something tragic will happen to test them, or that God will send them against their will, to some remote section of the world as a missionary to some savage tribe.

These and many other experiences of defeat have kept Christians from experiencing the joy of the Spirit-filled life. For example, do any of the following apply to you?

> An exalted feeling of your own importance
> Love of human praise
> Anger and impatience
> Self-will, stubborness, unteachability
> A compromising spirit
> Jealous disposition
> Lustful, unholy actions
> Dishonesty
> Unbelief
> Selfishness
> Love of money, beautiful clothes, cars, houses and land

Some of you may wonder, "Is it necessary for me to gain victory over all of my defeats and frustrations before I can be filled with the Holy Spirit?" Absolutely not! Just as Jesus Christ is the only one who can forgive your sins, so the Holy Spirit is the only one who can give victory and power.

HOW CAN A CHRISTIAN BE FILLED WITH THE HOLY SPIRIT?

It should be made clear that to be "filled with the Spirit" does not mean that we receive more of the Holy Spirit, but that we give Him more of ourselves. As we yield our lives to the Holy Spirit and are filled with His presence, He has greater freedom to work in and through our lives, to control us in order to better exalt and glorify Christ.

God is too great to be placed in a man-made mold. However, there are certain spiritual laws that are inviolate. Since the Holy Spirit already dwells within every Christian, it is no longer necessary to "wait in Jerusalem" as Jesus instructed the disciples to do, except to make personal preparation for His empowering. The Holy Spirit will fill us with His power the moment we are fully yielded.

I do not want to suggest that the following steps are the only way in which one can be filled with the Holy Spirit. This spiritual formula simply is offered, first, because it is scriptural, and second, because I know from experience that it works.

Do you want to be filled with the Holy Spirit? What are your motives? Are you looking for some ecstatic experience, or do you sincerely desire to serve the Lord Jesus Christ with greater power and effectiveness? Do you want, with all of your heart, to help others find Christ?

If so, then this is the spiritual formula that I urge you to consider prayerfully:

A. *We are commanded to be filled with the Spirit.*

"And do not get drunk with wine, for that is dissipation, but be filled with the Spirit" (Ephesians 5:18). This is an admonition of God. Do you think that He would ask you to do something beyond that which you are able to experience?

B. *We shall receive power for witnessing when we are filled.*

"But you shall receive power when the Holy Spirit has come upon you; and you shall be My witnesses both in Jerusalem, and in all Judea and Samaria, and even to the remotest part of the earth" (Acts 1:8). Why do we need power? To be Christ's witnesses right where we are and in the remotest part of the earth. Can your sincerely say that this is your motive for wanting to be filled with the Spirit?

C. *If any man is thirsty, let him come to Me and drink.*

"Now on the last day, the great day of the feast, Jesus stood and cried out, saying, If any man is thirsty, let him come to Me and drink. He who believes in Me, as the Scripture said, "From his innermost being shall flow rivers of living water." But this He spoke of the Spirit...not yet given, because Jesus was not yet glorified" (John 7:37-39). When a Christian is ready to respond to the gracious invitation of our blessed Savior, he is ready to relinquish his will for the will of God.

Therefore, this third step involves a complete surrender of your will, without reservation, to the will of God. The challenge of Romans 12:1,2 has become clear and meaningful to you and you want to "...present your body a living and holy sacrifice, acceptable to God, which is your spiritual service of worship." And you no longer want to be conformed to this world, but you want to be transformed by the renewing of your mind, "that you may prove what the will of God is, that which is good and acceptable and perfect."

You know that your body is the temple of the Holy Spirit who lives within you. You are not your own anymore for you were bought with the precious blood of the Lord Jesus; therefore, you now want to glorify God in your body and in your spirit, which are God's (1 Corinthians 6:19,20).

D. *We appropriate the filling of the Holy Spirit by faith.*

Remember that, if you are a Christian, the Father, Son and Holy Spirit are already living within you. Great spiritual power and resources are available to you.

In Ephesians 5:18, Paul admonishes, "And do not get drunk with wine, for that is dissipation, but be filled with the Spirit."

Further, in 1 John 5:14, 15, we are assured, "And this is the confidence which we have before Him, that, if we ask anything according to His will, He hears us. And if we know that He hears us in whatever we ask, we know that we have the requests which we have asked from Him." We know that it is God's will that we be filled with His Spirit. Therefore, as we ask the Holy Spirit to fill us, we can know according to the Word of God that our prayer is answered.

Here is a review of the steps that we have discussed in preparation for the filling of the Holy Spirit:
1. We are admonished to be filled.
2. We are promised power for service when we are filled.
3. We are to yield our will to God's will and seek first the kingdom of God.
4. We are to appropriate the filling of the Holy Spirit by faith.

E. *We must expect to be filled.*

"And without faith it is impossible to please Him, for he who comes to God must belive that He is, and that He is a rewarder of those who seek Him" (Hebrews 11:6).

Do you believe God wants you to be filled with the Holy Spirit?

Do you believe God has the power to fill you with the Holy Spirit?

Find a quiet place where you can be alone and read again the portions of Scripture given in the preceding paragraphs. You do not have to wait for the Holy Spirit. He is already dwelling within you if you are a Christian. He is waiting for you to allow Him to fill you. Remember, "Be it done to you according to your faith." "He is a rewarder of those who seek Him."

We are filled with the Holy Spirit by faith alone. However, true prayer is one way of expressing your faith. The following is a suggested prayer:

"Dear Father, I need You. I acknowledge that I have been directing my own life and that, as a result, I have sinned against You. I thank You that You have forgiven my sins through Christ's death on the cross for me. I now invite Christ to again take His place on the throne of my life. Fill me with the Holy Spirit as You commanded me to be filled, and as You promised in Your Word that You would do if I asked in faith. I pray this in the name of Jesus. As an expression of my faith, I now thank You for directing my life and for filling me with the Holy Spirit."

Does this prayer express the desire of your heart? If so, bow in prayer and trust God to fill you with Holy Spirit right now.

HOW CAN A CHRISTIAN KNOW WHEN HE IS FILLED WITH THE HOLY SPIRIT?

There are two very good ways of knowing when you are filled with the Holy Spirit.

First, by the promises of the Word of God. And second, by personal experience.

Have you honestly yielded your life to Christ, your will to His will?

Do you believe that you are filled with the Holy Spirit at this moment? If so, thank Him that you are filled. Thank Him for His indwelling presence and power. Thank Him by faith for victory over defeat and for effectiveness in witnessing. Praise God and give thanks continually (Ephesians 5:20; 1 Thessalonians 5:18).

If you have faithfully yielded to the will of God and sincerely surrendered your way to Him in accordance with the steps outlined in this presentation, if you have asked Him to fill you — He has done it! "And this is the confidence which we have before Him, that, if we ask anything according to His will, He hears us. And if we know that He hears us in whatever we ask, we know that we have the requests which we have asked from Him" (1 John 5:14,15). Is it His will that you be filled, according to Ephesians 5:18? Then, can you believe that He has heard you? Now can you know that you have the petitions that you desired of Him?

God's Word promises us that we can know. Therefore, on the basis of His Word you can know that you are filled, if you have met the conditions which are given in His Word.

APPENDIX II

Financial Management Resources

Christianomics. This extensive study course is down to earth, very entertaining and loaded with practical financial helps. Author Jim Jackson helps you use all that God has given to you by earning all you can, saving all you can, and giving away all you can. The 330-page textbook is not available apart from being a registered student of the *Christianomics* course.

For more information, write:

Here's Life Resource Centers
Christianomics Study Course
2700 Little Mountain Drive
San Bernardino, CA 92414
Phone: 714-886-9711

Christian Financial Concepts. Founded by Larry Burkett, this organization has developed excellent seminars and written materials on money management. It also offers tips, economic perspective and insights that are well worth reading.

For more information, write:

Christian Financial Concepts
Route 5
Dahlonega, GA 30533
Phone: 404-864-4570

Christian Financial Management. Founded by Ron Blue, this firm consists of highly competent financial experts who specialize in helping Christians maximize their resources through wise training, counsel, analysis and money management.

For more information, write:

Christian Financial Management
5780 Peachtree Dinwoody Road NE
Suite 595
Atlanta, GA 30342
Phone: 404-255-0147

Another recognized financial consultant is Dick Bruso, president of Prestige Financial Planning, Inc., and author of the new book, *Help and Hope for Your Finances* (Here's Life Publishers). He has an extensive background in financial planning and tax, insurance and estate counseling, and he pioneered the idea of a financial "blueprint" based on biblical principles.

For more information, write:

Prestige Financial Planning, Inc.
4380 South Syracuse St.
Suite 307
Denver, CO 80237
Phone: 303-694-0555

The Great Commission Foundation. This ministry of Campus Crusade for Christ International offers excellent Christian counseling in handling your needs for trusts, uni-trusts, land gifts, wills, estates or annuities. All financial information is kept totally confidential. Many millions of dollars have been put to work in Kingdom business because of the assistance of the Great Commission Foundation staff.

I encourage you to write today for a free "Wills Preparation Guide." This will help you as you arrange an appointment with a Christian attorney. Write:

Great Commission Foundation
Arrowhead Springs 90-00
San Bernardino, CA 92414
(714) 886-9711

NOTES

Chapter 1
1. *Emerging Trends*, Princeton, NJ: Princeton Religion Research Center, Vol. 2, No. 10 (December 1980).
2. Thompson, Barbara R., interview with chaplain Richard Halverson, "Evangelicals' Subtle Infection," *Christianity Today* (November 12, 1982), p. 47.

Chapter 2
1. Prayer attributed to St. Francis of Assisi (1181-1226).
2. Bonham, Tol D., *God Doesn't Want Your Money*, Oklahoma City: Vary Idea Press, 1975, p. 28.

Chapter 3
1. James, Theodore, Jr., "Teen Formula Eludes Disney," *The Wall Street Journal* (June 23, 1980), p. 25.
2. "Introducing Touchstone Films," advertisement in *USA Today* (February 24, 1984), p. 6D.

Chapter 6
1. Ardala, Thomas R., *Hearst Castle—San Simeon*, New York: Hudson Hills Press, 1981, p. 229.
2. Ingles, David, "He's More Than Enough." (Published by David Ingles Music, P. O. Box 1924, Tulsa, OK, 74101, © 1978. Used by permission.)

Chapter 9
1. Bright, Bill, "How to Insure a Bountiful Harvest," *Worldwide Challenge* (September 1981), p. 5.

Chapter 10
1. From Bernie May letter, Wycliffe Bible Translators, November 1981.

Chapter 13
1. "We Gave 8% More in '83," *USA Today* (July 2, 1984), p. 1.
2. From a speech by David Jackson, *Los Angeles Times* (June 1, 1981), p. 25.

SCRIPTURE INDEX